Border Collies

Border Collies

Joan Bray

Kangaroo Press

Acknowledgments

A book such as this is never the work of one person. Though I may have penned the words and accept all responsibility, the input has come from many people and sources over years of involvement with dogs and not the least from the dogs themselves. I wish to acknowledge with thanks all those unnamed people who have assisted me along the way. A number of people have been more directly concerned with the production of this book. I am particularly indebted to Jane and Andrew Carrington whose constant encouragement and hours of typing of the (sometimes illegible) handwritten manuscript ensured that this book came to fruition. I also wish to thank Lisa Brack for the line diagrams and drawings which so clearly illustrate the text, the RASKC (now NSWCC) for their cooperation and my whole family for coping with 'mother and her dogs'!

Photographs: The photographs used throughout this book are intended to illustrate particular aspects of the characteristics of the Border Collie. It is not my intention to promote any particular type or breeder's kennel. I am especially appreciative of those people who agreed to the use of their photographs showing faults as well as desirable qualities, without any thought of their own gain. Most dogs used in the photographs are purposely left unnamed. The exceptions to this are the photographs used in Chapter 7, which are of dogs either deceased or from kennels no longer functional. As these dogs are part of the ancestry of much of the current stock of Borders, an identifiable photographic record is obviously desirable. I appreciate that the dogs included are only a very small part of the breed's ancestry and that many great and important dogs have not been included. This was purely the result of limited space and the intention that this publication be a functional handbook. No value judgment is intended.

I sincerely thank the following people for the provision of photographs: P. & R. Anderson, J. & L. Birch, L. Brooks, P. Buckley, J. & S. Causer, C. & T. Cavanagh, K. & M. Kelly, D. & P. Martin, D. Scott, C. Bradley, C. & G. Reade, J. & C. Sillince, S. Jones, D. Marquette, M. Thompson, I. Combe, J. Bray. Also Samantha Foster for the frontispiece and Iris Combe for the loan of her X-ray photographs of the skeletal system of a Border Collie. Any omission is unintentional.

Cover photograph courtesy Barbara Killworth

Reprinted 1995
This edition first published in 1993 by Kangaroo Press Pty Ltd
3 Whitehall Road Kenthurst NSW 2156 Australia
P.O. Box 6125 Dural Delivery Centre NSW 2158
Printed in Hong Kong through Colorcraft Ltd

ISBN 0 86417 555 8

Contents

The Border Collie is an all-rounder—show dog, companion dog, working dog, pet. These photographs portray show and obedience dogs at home: dog and rabbit enjoying each other's company, a dog socialising with his boy, and a Border in a slow creep, using 'eye' on a fowl

1 Beginning in Borders

So you have acquired or are considering getting your first Border Collie puppy! If you have purchased from a reputable breeder then your expectations should be of unquestioned intelligence, a gentle, loyal nature and a dog that is easy to live with!

The Border Collie is a very special breed (not unique, of course—every breed has certain qualities which appeal to different people), but the Border is the all-rounder of the dog world. A Border makes an excellent housedog, a good protector of people and property, a top show dog, is outstanding in obedience and sheepdog trialling and on top of all those accomplishments Borders are still out there doing the job they were bred to do—working stock! It is worth noting that very few breeds of dog are still primarily doing the task for which they were first bred; that the Border Collie is still doing so is part of its special appeal. To maintain these qualities in the Border is, I believe, *the* most important responsibility of breeders, judges and owners.

As the owner or potential owner of a Border Collie puppy, how can you ensure that it achieves its potential for the next 12 or 15 years? As a long-time Border Collie devotee and breeder I have been asked very similar questions over and over again about the care, raising, training and breeding of Border Collies. This chapter deals with general care procedures for the puppy, adult and aged dog and endeavours to cover the most commonly asked questions and simple health problems.

The puppy: 6 weeks to 1 year

For a puppy to grow into a sound, healthy adult, attention must be given to diet, rest and exercise, stimulation, social contact and training (see Chapter 3).

Diet

A weaned puppy, 6–8 weeks old, has a very small stomach but at the same time is growing rapidly, therefore needs small, frequent feeds. A suggested diet chart appears on the next page.

As puppies vary in size, capacity and appetite, you may find that your puppy requires slightly more than the amount suggested at times; if food is left in his bowl, the puppy may be satisfied with slightly less. The best guide is the individual puppy. If a puppy is full of energy (during play periods), has a healthy coat and appearance and firm motions you are probably feeding him correctly. However, there are some pitfalls:

Over-eating This results in a bloated appearance and excessive bowel motions. If overfeeding continues the older puppy carrying excess weight can develop structural problems such as splayed fronts; in the adult dog over-feeding causes poor health, lethargy, whelping problems and a shortened life.

It is important with this type of puppy not to develop the habit of continuously feeding the puppy 'treats'. Try to work out what the puppy's daily food requirement is, keeping in mind his growing stages, condition and weight and do not feed him more than he needs. Suitable amounts for an average Border puppy have been included in the chart. As suggested there, gradually reduce the number of feedings given per day. Adult dogs and puppies which have reached the age of 9–12 months require, and do best on, only one feed a day.

Not eating There are two common reasons for this problem.

1. The first problem is the slightly over-anxious pup whose main aim in life is to be with and please its owner. The working instincts are usually very strong in this type of Border which mostly ends up as a very loyal

Guide to Raising a Puppy

Address:

Phone No.:

Congratulations on choosing a Border Collie to share your life! I hope he/she gives you many hours of pleasure and loyal companionship! Following is a suggested guide for the care and feeding of your puppy, aimed at ensuring a strong healthy adult.

Name: *Date of Birth:*
Vaccinated: 1.   *Due:* 2.   3.
Wormed: *Due:*

Worming should continue at 3 monthly intervals thereafter, for the health of your dog and yourself and family.

Diet: Small, frequent meals are preferable for young puppies, gradually reducing to one meal a day for the adult dog. Meals are best given before a rest period, never before exercise or play.

6–12 weeks
Breakfast: cereal (e.g. ½–1 Weetbix); egg yolk (2–3 weekly), calcium
Lunch: soaked dry puppy food (e.g. Lucky Puppy)
Mid-afternoon: milk substitute, dry biscuits for dogs
Tea: 100 g mince meat, scraps (e.g. cheese, gravy, fruit, etc.)

3–6 months
Breakfast: soaked dry complete dog food (not kibble) or substitute boiled brown rice
Lunch: Biscuits or Goodos etc., milk/substitute
Tea: Meat mixed with complete dry dog food or brown rice, scraps, calcium

6–9 months
Breakfast: biscuits or Goodos
Tea: Dry dog food or brown rice mixed with meat & scraps, calcium, egg yolk (1 or 2 weekly)

9 months onwards
evening meal only as previously; approximate quantities 2 cups dry food, 1 cup meat, calcium no longer necessary.

The above is only a guide; obviously dogs vary in their appetite and growth rate. Your puppy should appear firm and healthy and be alert and active. An overweight dog is not a healthy dog and it is better not to allow your pet to develop the habit of seeking titbits. If you find your puppy leaving food in the dish, remove it and reduce that feeding accordingly. If puppy appears ribby or listless then he may need extra food or worming.

Exercise: As with a baby, puppies need some play periods and lots of sleep periods. Do not wake very young puppies indiscriminately. However, as puppies grow up their rest periods reduce, while an adult Border Collie needs regular, stimulating exercise, e.g. a long run, ball play, swimming.

Teething: While puppy's teeth are shedding he will want to chew continuously. Provide him with chew objects, e.g. large marrow bones (never chop, chicken or fish bones), hard, dry puppy biscuits, a piece of leather, etc. Do not allow puppy to chew plastic, e.g. pegs, flower pots, toys, as they can splinter and cause intestinal damage. Puppy may enjoy a play with a squeaky toy or ball but substitute a bone when he starts to chew.

Training: You will soon become aware that a Border Collie is a very intelligent dog. He therefore needs constant stimulation and will learn quickly. Give your Border as much responsibility as possible. Teach him to carry things (e.g. your bag or basket), pick up things, find things. If possible enrol him in an Obedience Training School.

and protective adult and a good, keen worker, e.g. in obedience or with stock. For this type of pup, food is of secondary importance. On the other hand, to ensure a well-boned adult dog, adequate feeding is essential during the puppy's growing stage. So a compromise has to be reached. I would suggest the following:

(a) Put the pup on an appetite stimulant such as Incremen or Energel.

(b) Feed the puppy in a situation where he can see you but where you can still continue to do your chores, e.g. let the puppy eat in a corner of the kitchen while you wash up. (Never stay and wait while the puppy eats as this leads to ongoing problems.) You may find that when you leave the room the puppy will quickly follow. This is OK. Simply return to where the puppy's food is, encourage him back to the bowl and return to your normal activities.

(c) Always remove the feed dish (after a reasonable time) whether the pup is finished or not. It is best not to leave food available non-stop as this only encourages the pup to 'pick and choose', to follow you around and occasionally nibble. Try to feed the puppy in the same spot and at the same time each day as this will build up his confidence.

2. The second problem is the pup which is training its owner to pander to it to gain extra attention. I have known many clever Borders who have trained their owners to feed them only something special, such as freshly cooked chicken meat! Others have trained their carers to sit beside them and actually feed them bit by bit! Then there was the clever dog who trained his owner to play roll-over-and-catch games with his food! In each case the dogs have managed to gain hours of the owner's time and attention under the guise of being disinterested eaters.

Unnecessary feeding problems begin where owners become convinced that *their* dog won't eat (or won't eat dog food).

When dealing with this type of puppy, keep in mind that *a normal, healthy pup will not starve itself to death.*

I have found the best way to deal with picky eaters is not to add any titbits but to reduce the amount of dry food in the bowl (say to about one third of a normal feeding) and to lock the pup away with this for the night. Under these circumstances the pup usually has a clean plate in the morning. You lose your anxieties about him not eating and he gradually settles down to a satisfactory eating pattern. Of course it may take a few nights to establish this pattern and then you can gradually (note *gradually*) increase the amount that you give him. It may be worthwhile during this period to give the puppy some vitamin tablets, e.g. Visorbits, given directly down the throat. You may decide to have the puppy checked by the vet to establish that it is fit and well and simply being a typical 'I'll try it on' Border Collie.

My belief is that food should simply be what is best to maintain your pet in good health, but that feeding time should never be the highlight of the dog's day. Being your companion, friend and guardian is far more important to the Border. Because of this (and because of the way a dog's digestive and absorption system functions) I have found the following regime most satisfactory for the adult Border (1 year and older):
• One feed a day in the late afternoon—after the dog has finished its exercise for the day, but giving it time to relieve itself before bedding down for the night.
• A combination of two-thirds dry complete dog food and one-third fresh meat—include table scraps, fruit, vegetables, etc. Try to vary the type or brand of kibble and type of meat.

A satisfactory alternative to commercial dry dog food is boiled brown rice, oatmeal, barley and vegetables mixed with fresh meat.

Diarrhoea in puppies

Dogs can suffer loose motions through a change of diet, even something so simple as a change in brand of dry food, extra rich foods or an excess of food. If puppy is still full of energy and acting normally simply follow the same procedure that you would for a human. Stop solid foods and milk, give plenty of glucose and water for 24 hours (make sure the puppy does drink as they can dehydrate quickly when very young), then re-introduce solid foods very slowly, in small quantities, perhaps starting with natural yoghurt. New foods are always best introduced slowly and mixed with something that the dog is already used to. Milk should always be diluted and used sparingly. I prefer a milk substitute, e.g. Denkavit, but follow your breeder's recommendations. Loose motions can also follow stress or situations that the puppy hasn't become accustomed to, e.g. travel, vaccinations. These usually require no special attention. However, loose motions can also result from various gut viruses or infections. You will normally recognise this type by an offensive smell and a listless, unhappy puppy. If a puppy begins to act very differently from normal, looks 'caved in' at the sides or perhaps begins to vomit or retch, then the best procedure is to contact a vet.

Rest

Just like babies, pups need lots of rest; it is important to provide them with a quiet place to which they can retreat to sleep undisturbed. Try not to allow people to continually disturb the puppy while it's resting and you will be rewarded with a strong, well adjusted adult dog. Eventually, of course, the pup will outgrow this need and will develop that marvellous trait of the canine species to rest 'tuned in' to their surroundings and to wake instantly alert at the sound of a car door or a stranger approaching.

Exercise

If given the opportunity, Border Collie pups will exercise themselves. As soon as they are on their feet (at about two weeks of age) they begin to wrestle with each other, to play crouch and pounce and to scamper along when they hear familiar sounds. Your puppy, probably now on his own, will continue in the same pattern—scampering around the yard or house, often finding and dragging around objects such as shoes or toilet brushes. He will climb and leap off lounges or doorsteps; he will continue to play crouch and leap, substituting your feet for another puppy. The puppy is instinctively developing survival skills following predetermined biological patterns, in much the same way as very young babies, as soon as they feel something in the hand, will take it straight to their mouth. Puppies under 3–4 months do not need long walks for exercise. Of course you will probably want to start their socialisation training but avoid putting a young puppy on a lead and forcing it to undergo long tiring walks.

Adult Border Collies do need plenty of exercise and this will depend upon your own environment—swimming, playing soccer or ball with an obliging friend and most of all just simply running. To my eye there are very few sights to compare with that of a strong, healthy Border Collie striding effortlessly across a paddock, grinning with sheer joy.

Many of our Borders are quite happy housed in backyards of varying sizes, although many backyards end up with a well worn track where the dog has simply found a way of exercising. In the absence of 'stock on the ground' (kids are a great substitute here—your Border is quite happy herding and circling any children who might be playing in the yard), I have known many Borders to herd birds, i.e. watching the birds fly overhead and chasing them as far as the backyard will allow.

Socialisation: six week old puppies
with household pet rabbit

By about 4–5 months, begin taking the puppy for a walk (see next page, Lead training). If possible include a running free period, perhaps on a quiet beach, in a park or on a sports oval. Of course you will only be able to do this once the puppy has learnt to return to you when he is called.

By the age of 18 months a Border needs more exercise than you can give him by simply walking him around the block. If possible twenty minutes of running beside you on a pushbike would be a good substitute.

Toilet training

If a puppy is to be allowed inside it is important to train him not to mess in the house. There is no shortcut method of doing this as the puppy does not understand the difference between 'inside' and 'outside'. He is simply used to finding a quiet spot somewhere, normally away from his sleeping quarters, and using it. Your task is to train the puppy to find that spot outside! This requires you, when the puppy is inside, to watch him carefully and to learn to read the signs which will tell you when he wants to relieve himself. The most common signs are sniffing the floor, circling (looking for a spot), going off on his own behind a chair, into another room, etc. Normally after feeding, small puppies need to defaecate

(empty out), and after waking from a sleep puppies usually need to urinate.

Once you recognise when a puppy needs to relieve himself, take him to a particular spot outside and allow him to go to the toilet, giving a command such as 'drop it'. Always try to use the same spot as this will increase his awareness of what you require of him when you take him outside. Building up an association with a particular spot can be very useful later on, e.g. if you wish your adult dog to relieve himself before setting out on a journey. As always in training, once a puppy does what is required of him give him his praise reward.

Of course, to succeed in training a puppy this way requires an owner to keep a very close watch while the puppy is inside, especially for the first few weeks after he becomes a part of your family group. After a meal or drink, always take a very small puppy outside for a few minutes. If you are vigilant and consistent in watching your puppy he will learn only to relieve himself outside fairly quickly. If you neglect to watch carefully and the puppy has to relieve himself inside, he learns an undesirable behaviour which may take a lot longer to correct. If you find that you cannot watch constantly, then it is best to leave the puppy outside at those times. If you catch puppy *in the act* of messing inside, then a firm 'no!' is all that is required as you carry puppy outside as usual. Although you may feel annoyed, you must still give him his praise if he completes the action in the right place. Any more severe correction such as hitting him or rubbing his nose in the mess is definitely *not* recommended.

If you do not actually catch the puppy in the act, but find the mess later, no action can be taken except to watch puppy more carefully next time! However, the spot should be thoroughly cleaned and disinfected as dogs do tend to continue to use the same spot if they pick up a previous scent there.

If you wish to train your puppy to sleep inside at night you will need to start by keeping him in a very confined area, e.g. laundry or shower room. Cover the whole area with newspaper as a small puppy cannot possibly go through the night without relieving himself. However, you can help by taking him outside last thing at night and again very early in the morning. As they grow older, puppies gradually learn to wait until they are let out in the morning.

Lead training

Puppies do not take kindly to being restricted, as on the end of a lead, but for their own well-being it is preferable that they learn to adjust both to being tied-up and to walking on a lead at an early age. One way to start is to put a narrow soft collar (such as a cat collar) on your puppy when he is about 8 to 10 weeks old and allow him to adjust to the feel of something around his neck. After several days attach a short, narrow nylon or webbing lead to the collar and allow the puppy to trail it around for a few minutes each day for two or three days. Watch carefully at this time to make sure that the lead doesn't catch on any obstacles, such as fence posts, which could cause the puppy injury or discomfort. Finally, begin to catch on to the lead and move backwards, calling puppy towards you as though in a game. As puppy comes to you, encourage him and praise him. If the intention is to take up obedience training at a later date, then puppy should be gently manoeuvred to the left side for pats and praise.

To teach a puppy to walk down the street, the simplest method is to drive or carry the puppy to the end of your block (or some appropriate distance), clip on the lead, put the puppy on the ground and head for home! The chances are that puppy will quite enthusiastically run ahead of you towards the security of his own yard. Attempts to walk a puppy away from the area in which he feels safe usually result in his 'digging in' and refusing to move. This becomes

frustrating for the owner and usually ends up in a tugging match which becomes an unpleasant experience for the puppy. The main aim at this stage is to gradually teach the puppy that going for walks on a lead can be interesting and enjoyable.

If your aim is to have a well behaved adult dog then your puppy should begin his basic training as early as possible—any time from three or four weeks onwards. This begins as play training as outlined in Chapter 3.

(*Note:* If at any stage you begin to use a check chain for lead work make sure never to leave it on when the dog is unattended, as a check chain can very easily catch on fences, posts and branches and cause injury or death through strangulation.)

Socialisation

In much the same way as people, Border Collie puppies tend to have differing personalities: some are outgoing and boisterous, others shy or timid, gentle, affectionate, stand-offish or sensible. In all cases I believe that all puppies can benefit from socialisation training. Put simply, this means being taught to get along with people, other animals, objects and situations.

One would hope that by the time you take your puppy home his socialisation has already begun. In my own kennels the puppies are all handled from a very early age by all members of the household. By about 4 months of age it is helpful to have small children sharing a game with them.

Border Collies are known for their tolerance of the ways of small children but children should also be educated to handle puppies. I always insist that a child sit down to handle a puppy as they can very easily squirm out of a child's grasp and fall to the ground to end up with an injury. Children must be shown how to handle puppies gently and not to squeeze them or pull them by the limbs. (For more details on early socialisation see page 31.)

The new owner's part in the puppy's socialisation should start as soon as the puppy is taken home.

Encourage family and friends to pat and play with the puppy, especially timid puppies. If the puppy tends to back away restrain him gently (keep puppy on the ground or floor) and talk reassuringly while other people stroke the puppy gently on the chest. Avoid patting puppies on the head as this is an area of intimidation. It is better, if people are cooperative, to kneel down rather than bend over a puppy. On the other hand, if the puppy is boisterous and wants to jump up, encourage

A one year old bitch out of coat.

The same bitch matured and coming into coat

will tolerate visitors and regular callers but will still be protective when needed.

Whatever are to be the normal parts of your lifestyle should be introduced to the puppy while he is very young. If you intend to have your dog travel with you, then start by taking him on short car trips as a puppy. Put an old rug or towel over the seat in case of car sickness. If the puppy shows signs of car sickness after the first car ride then the following remedies may be tried:

• Half a junket tablet a short while before setting out to settle the tummy.

• Confine the pup so that he is not constantly moving around, e.g. in a pen or box or held on the knee.

• Allow the pup to gradually become accustomed to the unfamiliar movement of a car by starting with frequent, very short trips.

For further socialisation walk your puppy on a lead around shopping centres and along busy, noisy streets to introduce everyday noises such as trucks, buses, trains, crowds. Be gentle and reassuring as these can be frightening sounds to a small puppy.

Socialisation is a matter of commonsense and thinking ahead. Remember that a puppy which has come from a kennel-type situation may not be used to the sounds of common appliances such as vacuum cleaners and lawnmowers.

The adult dog

By the time a Border Collie is eighteen months old it should have reached its potential height of somewhere between 46–51 cm for a bitch (18–20 inches) and 48–53 cm (19–21 inches) for a dog. Bone structure and physical features are now well laid down and will not change significantly, though you may have observed certain changes taking place up to this point (see page 39, Stages of Development).

The young dog or bitch will continue to fill out and mature until the age of three years. In fact, the maturity rate between different strains or bloodlines causes variations as well. Maturity and chest development is hastened in a dog used at stud; their approach to life becomes bolder and more assertive at this time as well. A male usually has his adult type of coat by the age of two years and, apart from an annual moult, this changes very little.

The bitch, on the other hand, will mature after a

him into the sit position (see page 46) before handling him.

The concern most people have with socialisation is: will the adult dog still be protective? My experience has been that a dog bonds to you and your property and

The bitch from the previous page as an overweight matron (showing her non-collar side)

litter but tends to become more placid and loyal to her family and surroundings. Subsequent breeding results in a decidedly 'matronly' appearance and approach to life. The bitch's coat is more difficult to stabilise, being affected by hormonal changes associated with her heat period and whelpings.

If play training, limitation training and socialisation have continued from an early age your adult dog should now be responding readily to commands, under control and know its place in the family pack.

It must be pointed out that under different circumstances, the age of eighteen months to two years would be about the time that a working Border Collie would be expected to commence serious stockwork and therefore it is natural for your dog, at this time, to become quite active and in need of stimulation and exercise. It may be that you have already commenced showing your Border or have joined an obedience training club. This, combined with continuous involvement at home, should result in a happy, well-adjusted dog. On the other hand, you may not be interested in either of these two pursuits and may simply wish to keep your dog as a family pet. In this case I would suggest that a real effort is made to give your adult Border a lot of hard exercise, preferably daily but otherwise 2–3 times a week. Depending upon your lifestyle suggestions include:
• Accompanying a family member while jogging or bike riding
• A morning and evening brisk walk (2–3 km)
• Free run on a beach or in a park (Council permitting)
• Swimming: beach, dam, creek or private pool (I have known several happy Borders to accompany their owners surfing and surfboard riding)
• Play periods of chasing a tennis ball, family soccer, fetching a stick, etc.

Treated with discipline and as a part of the family structure and outings, the Border will fit happily into the family pet situation and should prove to be a loyal and devoted protector of family and property. When treated well, Border Collies very rarely roam, preferring to remain at home for guard duty. At the approach of strangers a Border will normally sound a warning growl and if necessary 'hold', i.e. grasp clothing or limbs by the mouth, but they very rarely bite. If the warnings are ignored then a nip may be given, though in my experience this very rarely results in breaking the skin.

A Border which takes to wandering or chasing cars is usually one with an extremely well-developed working instinct. It may be kinder in the long run to place this type of dog on a farm.

By and large, the Border is an easy dog to care for and own, but there are some commonly occurring conditions which it is as well for the Border owner to be aware of. These are outlined on pages 15–17.

The old dog

Barring accidents, a well-cared for Border Collie usually lives to the age of 12–15 years (in some cases longer). Bitches used for breeding, though, may succumb to

The Border Collie
at his peak—fit,
active and enjoying
life

cancer of the uterus or mammary glands at around 11 or 12 years. Parasitic infestation, e.g. heartworm, may also shorten your dog's life.

Border Collies usually remain quite active almost until their life's end. The signs you may pick up on that your dog is aging will be such things as grey flecking in the muzzle and around the eyes, stiffness of joints, the onset of arthritis and difficulty in rising, longer periods of rest and deeper sleep, i.e. the dog doesn't wake as quickly with the approach of a car or stranger, a 'browning-off' or dryness to the coat, loss of teeth, diminished hearing and eyesight, loss of interest in food, lower tolerance levels, incontinence, and pyometra (uterine infection).

Obviously, these signs indicate the need for some changes to be made to make your companion's old age more comfortable. These changes may be grouped into three areas—health and exercise, interest and comfort.

Health and exercise

Old dogs sometimes begin to lose an interest in food and exercise. It is important to maintain a good diet and not to allow the old dog to develop into a finicky eater of foods which will result in it becoming overweight. Thus, resist the temptation to tempt your old dog with 'people' food such as biscuits, fatty chicken, bread and the like. Continue a normal diet of dry dog food and meat though perhaps reducing the quantities. If your dog's teeth are affected then the kibble may need to be soaked in warm water or gravy and the meat may need to be chopped or minced. Include a vitamin supplement.

Lack of the desire to exercise, if left unchecked, may also lead to an overweight, lethargic dog. Of course, the old dog's exercise should be reduced in time and strenuousness. Gentler walks may be indicated though swimming, if your dog enjoys it, is still satisfactory.

The older dog should have an annual check-up from the vet who will monitor such things as removing problem teeth; clean ears; eye problems and pyometra in bitches. Recognise that your old dog will feel the cold and provide warm undercover sleeping quarters. An old dog shivering in the wet or cold conditions is a sad sight and a disgrace to the owner.

Interest

Continue to foster your old dog's interest in life. Though he may be well past his show or obedience career, continue to groom him and take him on outings; enter Veterans' parades or continue to practise simple obedience exercises. Especially if you have younger dogs,

The old lady—enjoying the special privileges and attention she deserves

make sure your old boy or girl is not neglected. Though your dog may begin to show signs of incontinence (loss of bladder control) treat him with understanding and help him to retain his dignity.

Comfort

The older dog may become a little less tolerant of rough handling, especially by children, and this is best explained to youngsters accustomed to playing with your dog. The old dog should not be disturbed when resting. Provide warm comfortable sleeping quarters and soft bedding if your dog is arthritic. Recognise that the dog may have diminished hearing and eyesight. He may not respond quickly to your commands simply because he cannot hear you. Check ears and teeth regularly, clip nails and keep the dog's coat free of matting and tangles.

Finally, recognise when the time comes to say farewell to your friend of 12 years or more and allow him to die with dignity and freedom from pain and stress.

Simple common problems

Skin problems

Border Collies occasionally develop one or other of several different types of skin disorders:
• Dry, flaky skin and loss of hair
• A bald, raw patch at the base of the tail which the dog continuously attempts to scratch, which usually, as a result, worsens. This occurs mostly in hot weather and is often termed 'summer eczema' or 'hot spots'.

The causes of these various skin disorders may be one or a combination of factors:
• Flea irritation causes the dog to scratch excessively and allow infections to develop.
• Food, flea or grass allergies.
• Excess fat in the diet, especially combined with hot weather and a thick coat.
• Bacterial infection.

Skin problems are irritating and unsightly rather than debilitating, especially as they require constant attention to keep under control. Some suggested approaches include:
• Ensure the dog remains free of fleas; check sleeping area and bedding.
• Reduce the intake of fat, especially with the onset of hot weather. This may require changing your brand of complete dry dog food to one with a lower fat content or, if the problem is severe, alter the dog's diet to boiled rice, vegetables and a minimum of lean meat; include a vitamin supplement.
• Treat the skin by bathing the dog fortnightly throughout summer with a fungicidal or medicated shampoo, e.g. Triocil, Derma-wash or ti-tree oil.
• Apply soothing lotions such as calamine to deter the dog scratching; for wet eczema use a drying agent such as Ectasol.

Breeders should note that it is believed that a predisposition to skin disorders involves heritable factors.

Therefore, breeding together dogs known to suffer from 'hot spots' or 'summer eczema' is certainly compounding the problem in the offspring.

Collie nose

An acute sensitivity to sunlight in some dogs of the Collie breed means that the nose (even though it may be completely pigmented) and muzzle may become sunburnt and blistered. This condition worsens with each subsequent summer season. Some suggested methods of easing the problem include the constant use of sunscreen lotions or creams, and tattooing (check with a vet).

Constipation

This usually results from feeding a dog too many bones or from a loss of muscle tone in an older dog.

If a dog appears 'not himself', listless, not interested in food, then check for constipation. Often the dog will strain and hunch in an attempt to defaecate; when the dog does defaecate, it may be with pain and difficulty. The stool will usually appear hard and chalk-like and whitish in colour. If detected early enough a tablespoon of paraffin oil is a suitable remedy.

Diarrhoea

Not common, diarrhoea may result from a change of diet, too much rich food such as full cream milk, a change in water, e.g. when travelling, the excessive eating of animal manure, as a result of enteritis caused by bacteria or parasites (worm infestation) or from extreme constipation.

Dietary diarrhoea usually responds to 24–36 hours of starvation but allow the dog water or water and glucose (if travelling the water may have to be boiled). A proprietary anti-diarrhoeal such as Kaopectate or Scourban could also be tried. Reintroduce food in very small quantities, preferably something bland such as boiled rice.

Diarrhoea caused by an infection or severe worm infestation requires veterinary attention. It may be recognised by an offensive smell, blood in the motions, pale anaemic gums, and the dog becoming listless, wobbly on his feet or having a temperature.

(*Note:* A dog's normal temperature is within the range 37.5°C to 38.8°C and is taken using a rectal thermometer inserted into the anus and held in position for 2 minutes.)

Unwanted mating

Unless a bitch has been desexed, extreme care must be taken during the whole three weeks of her heat period to prevent an unplanned mating occurring. However, if you do find your bitch tied to an obliging, uninvited dog, your vet can give her an appropriate 'mismate' injection to prevent the pregnancy continuing, providing the vet is consulted within 24 hours of the tie occurring. It should be noted that this will prolong the heat period and the bitch will continue to be vulnerable.

Consideration should be given to desexing any dog to be kept as a pet, male or female. This involves removing the ovaries in bitches (spaying) and testicles in males so that the animal becomes incapable of producing offspring. The advantages of doing this are:
- It prevents accidental matings taking place.
- It makes the animals less likely to wander or fight.
- It removes the need to lock up a bitch during heat periods.
- It generally has a calming effect.

After desexing care must be taken to ensure that the dog exercises regularly and is not allowed to overeat as there is often a problem with desexed animals becoming overweight.

Weight control

Obesity

Commonsense should prevail in cases of obesity; an overweight dog is not a healthy animal and is subject to whelping problems and a shortened lifespan. The cause of a dog's weight problem is always with the owner, usually poor diet, the constant feeding of titbits, and lack of exercise.

Initially the dog will need a weight-reducing diet combined with an increase in exercise; once the weight has returned to a desirable level then correct feeding and exercise (as outlined elsewhere) should be maintained.

One suggestion for a weight-reducing diet is to cut out all commercial dog foods and feed the adult dog 1½ cups of boiled brown rice and 'water' vegetables, e.g. cauliflower, cabbage, celery. This may be made more appetising by including a stock cube for flavour. It may be necessary to give the dog a vitamin supplement as well and perhaps 250 grams of very lean meat once a week.

Underweight

Many Border Colies are very, very active and despite careful feeding maintain themselves in healthy, hard, muscular condition. If the dog is fit and active then being slightly lean should not be a problem.

However, if the dog is obviously ribby, has a dry, harsh coat, lacks a sparkle to the eyes or lacks energy, then a food absorption problem may be indicated. Possible causes are worm infestation, vitamin deficiency, or the inability of the dog's digestive system to absorb certain foods.

If the dog has been regularly wormed, has been receiving a correct diet including adequate vitamins and (if poor eating patterns has caused the problem) has been tried on an appetite stimulant, then the dog may need to be checked by a vet who will determine the cause of the problem and prescribe the correct treatment.

Anal irritation

Dogs are sometimes observed dragging their bottom along the ground in an action known as 'skidding'. The most common causes for this are worm infestation or an infection or blockage in the anal glands. If worming does not appear to relieve the problem then the dog's anal glands may have to be cleaned out or expressed. A vet will do this though many dog owners learn to perform this task successfully with practice.

Worming and immunisation

Routine worming and vaccinating should continue over the whole of your dog's lifetime. Requirements will vary according to the medication used and the particular problems associated with the area in which the dog lives. Your vet will advise you on this.

2 Breeding and Raising a Litter

Owners of purebred Border Collies often consider, at some stage, the question of allowing their bitch to be mated or their dog to be used at stud. By and large, breeders fall into one of three categories.

The occasional breeder

Having acquired a beautiful pedigree bitch, it is very natural for new owners to want her to have a litter. This is usually to satisfy their own curiosity or for the education of their children or even in the hope of recouping their purchase price. This type of owner most often genuinely has the bitch as a pet and will breed maybe two or at the most three litters from her. They may or may not be involved in showing or obedience training. This type of breeder usually does their very best to sell sound, healthy puppies.

'The backyarder'

The 'backyard breeder' runs one or two bitches and one dog. The bitches are often mated on each season to the same dog. This type of breeder contributes very little to the breed, never being involved in showing, promoting or improving the breed. The 'backyarder' appears to be more interested in cashing in on the popularity of the dog. Sadly, their puppies are often sold unvaccinated, inadequately wormed and in poor condition.

The kennel breeder

The kennel breeder has probably built up stock over many years of involvement in showing, promoting and improving the breed and indeed in establishing their own particular line. The kennel breeder will usually run eight or more dogs, including possibly two stud dogs, and will usually be heavily involved in the dog world. Kennel breeders are usually 'running-on' young stock both to maintain their involvement in exhibiting (shows, trials) and to replace ageing stock and maintain their line. This group would possibly breed two or more litters a year, selling well-cared-for puppies. (Suggestions for establishing a kennel line are made in Chapter 6.)

The novice breeder

A step-by-step guide

Should I let my bitch have a litter?
Provided the bitch is well bred, sound and healthy with no major heritable faults and provided you wish to have the experience of breeding a litter, then the answer is 'yes'. Of course you will have carefully considered the expense and work involved and the need to find good homes for 6 to 8 puppies.

Should I let my bitch have a litter before she is desexed?
If you simply wish to breed a litter before having your bitch desexed, you must realise that this may take up to two years and is not necessary for the bitch's wellbeing.

At what age should my bitch have her first litter?
My advice would be not before the age of two years, depending on when she first comes into season. As a rule of thumb Border Collies tend to have their first real

oestrus cycle between 11 and 13 months, and then at around seven-monthly intervals. Occasionally early-maturing lines have been known to start around 6 or 7 months. Sometimes a young bitch will have 2 or 3 days 'show' of blood before a complete oestrus cycle occurs some months later. I would not put a bitch into whelp on her first season, so that her first mating should be around two years and probably not later than the age of three years. (See page 95, Ceroid-lipofusinosis.)

How can I arrange a mating?
If you have purchased your puppy through a reputable breeder, that breeder is the best person to advise you on the choice of a stud dog and to assist you in the arranging of the mating. Your alternative is to attend several recognised dog shows and to get to know other breeders and what dogs are available.

If you are to breed a pedigreed, registered litter you will need to be a member of the Kennel Control in your state and to have applied for a breeder's prefix. Of course, you would need to have had the bitch's registration papers transferred into your ownership.

What dog should I use?
Again, if you have obtained your puppy from a reputable breeder, then the breeder would be the person most familiar with the background of your bitch and therefore best able to advise you on a suitable mate for her. If, however, you have begun to be interested in breeding yourself and you wish to select your own stud dog, see page 20.

What are the costs?
The major costs involved in producing a purebred, registered litter, assuming a normal, healthy whelping, are:
• Stud fee (approximately the same as the current market price for a registered puppy).
• Vet fees—swab, worming, vaccinations.
• Supplementary diet for bitch and puppies.
• Kennel Control costs—membership, breeder's prefix, registration.
• Advertising.

Before you start

The bitch in season
Whether you intend to breed or not, if you have a non-desexed bitch in your yard you should train yourself to watch for her coming into season. This really refers to the period of time in the oestrus cycle during which hormonal changes occur in the bitch enabling (indeed stimulating) her to become mated.

Very simply, the stages of the oestrus cycle are:
1. The preparation stage when bleeding occurs.
2. Ovulation—during which the ova are released into the Fallopian tubes. During this stage the discharge pales to straw-coloured.
3. Oestrus (true heat) when the bitch will accept the male.
4. Implantation—if a mating occurs fertilised ova are implanted in the lining of the uterus.

How do I check for a bitch in season?
You can check your bitch while she is either standing or lying down, but it is important to open the lips of the vulva and check carefully, perhaps applying a clean tissue to the area. Check for staining, as many bitches will lick themselves very clean. Because of this she should be checked morning and night. If the first thing you notice is blood around the sleeping quarters (or across the kitchen floor!) then chances are that she has already been in season for many days. Other signs you may pick up will be the lips of the vulva becoming enlarged, perhaps excessive licking of the vulval area, a good bloom to the coat and of course the response of male dogs.

Counting the days
Once you determine the first day of bleeding mark down the day as 'day 1'. It is best not to rely on your memory as you really want to be able to determine in the future the exact period of time between seasons. As dogs are reasonably regular, knowing when to start checking your bitch makes it easier to take the necessary steps to prevent unplanned whelpings. In any case, if you are to put your bitch into whelp you will need to be able to determine the days on which she is ready to accept a male.

Pre-mating procedures
1. Allow two oestrus cycles to run their full course before planning to mate your bitch.
2. Ensure the bitch is healthy and fit. By this I mean not overweight and in good muscle tone. (See section on whelping problems, page 36.)
3. Worm the bitch when she first comes into season.
4. You may wish to have a swab done or the owner of the stud dog may require a swab before allowing you the use of him. This means that your vet will take a scraping from the lining of the bitch's cervix and

test it for any signs of infection which might be transferred to the dog or affect the healthy development of the litter.

5. Select your stud dog and make the necessary arrangements with the owner, giving an approximate date when you will require his services.

Selecting the stud dog

It should always be remembered that whether you intend to become a kennel breeder or simply be an occasional breeder, your aim should be to produce sound, healthy puppies as free as possible from inheritable defects and maintaining the characteristics of the breed.

As far as possible, the stud dog and bitch should complement each other in their offspring, e.g. if you have a sound bitch with a very good coat, but a little on the small side, then her mate should be a dog known to throw good-sized puppies, even though he may have a mediocre coat.

It must be remembered, though, that each dog and bitch carry a very large pool of genetic possibilities and your only reliable guide to what you might expect in your puppies is not the dog you are looking at, but the progeny or offspring of that dog. I recall a new breeder, looking at her very first litter, phoning me up and asking: 'What did I do wrong? I put my perfectly marked bitch to a perfectly marked dog, but the markings of these puppies are terrible. There are only two reasonably marked pups in the whole litter!'

It is important to remember, when planning your mating, that your puppies should end up as much loved companions, either as pets, show or obedience dogs, and therefore a good nature and a true Border Collie temperament is of prime importance.

The Border Collie should be gentle and sweet natured, playful but long-suffering (especially with children) and under normal circumstances never aggressive. On the other hand, he is also very loyal and protective of his property (which includes his 'people').

As a rule of thumb for the inexperienced breeder, I should say never breed from a dog or bitch which shows any signs of having a bad or aggressive temperament. Sadly, puppies with a tendency to bad temperament usually cause a lot of heartache for somebody later on. I firmly believe that the renowned good nature of the Border Collie should always be maintained.

Alternative stud dog selection

1. Contact the Border Collie club in your state for a copy of their stud dog register. This will give you the names of the dogs and their owners' telephone numbers, and in some cases a profile of the dogs, i.e. the pedigree, photograph and characteristics they are known to throw. To locate your Border Collie club check with the breeder of your bitch or contact the Kennel Control Office in your state's capital city.

2. Attend several dog shows—carefully study the dogs being exhibited and talk to the owners. Take your bitch's pedigree with you. The first question you are sure to be asked is, 'What breeding is she?' Try not to be put off or offended by this as well-established breeders are usually fairly selective of the bitches they allow their dogs to be used over. This makes sense when you realise that their reputation as a breeder of good quality Border Collies is at stake. However, most breeders will be very helpful and discuss your particular case with you. If they feel that your line is not compatible with their own, they may be able to suggest an alternative for you.

3. Again, contact your state's Kennel Control for telephone numbers of breeders listed in their directory.

4. Ask your vet! He may well be the vet to other Border Collie owners in your district.

The experienced stud dog

Where possible it is preferable to take a maiden bitch (a bitch which has not been mated before) to a proven stud dog (a dog which has mated and produced puppies), what is called an 'old hand'. There are several reasons for this. Firstly, a maiden bitch can sometimes be fearful or 'flighty'. A good experienced stud dog can make the job a lot easier. Secondly, if no puppies ensue from the mating then chances are that the problem has to be found in the bitch, the dog having proven himself with previous litters. This is only a general guide, of course—a proven dog can have difficulties as well.

(*Note:* The same advice is generally given for the novice stud dog as well—that is, to start him off with a bitch which has previously mated and whelped.)

Determining the right day

By this time you have determined approximately when your bitch is due for her second or third season, selected your stud dog and made preliminary arrangements. How will you know when to take your bitch to the dog?

If your bitch is a maiden then a process of trial and error will be involved. It is usually, but not always, the case that a bitch will not accept a dog for mating unless she is 'ready'. Being ready means that the eggs are shedding and moving down the Fallopian tubes ready to be fertilised by the dog's sperm. It has been found that this occurs in most dogs somewhere between day 5 and 18, so that most breeders suggest trying for a mating on day 12 or 13. (Day 13 here refers to the 13th day of the oestrus cycle which you can count up from day 1, carefully noted down as explained earlier.) However, bitches have been known to produce puppies from matings as early as day 6 and as late as day 17, so the 12 or 13 day rule is a guide only.

There are several other signs which may help to find the correct day:
1. The discharge changes from red to straw-coloured (yellowish).
2. The vulva becomes very enlarged and moist.
3. The bitch stands and 'flags' her tail (lifts her tail in the air and swings it from side to side).
4. When gently stroked on the outside of her hind-leg (thigh) she will swing her tail to the side.
5. A vet can do tests to determine the correct day but this is generally not needed unless your bitch has had a previously unsuccessful mating.
6. The bitch's behaviour in front of a dog (and his behaviour in return!) is usually a good guide, but unless you have the stud dog in your own yard or kennels, this is generally not a practical proposition. There are very few breeders who would want a bitch brought to their dog more than two or three times in her season.

It cannot be stressed too strongly that there is no infallible way of determining when your bitch is ready for mating except to put her with a male dog from about day 6 onwards. Most stud dog owners will suggest a time somewhere between day 11 to day 14, as on average this appears to be a satisfactory time. Experience only enables you to be more accurate with your own bitch. If your bitch misses on your first try then, before her next heat period, have her checked by a Vet, simply to determine that she is fit and has no obvious problems. Then try earlier and/or later in the cycle. It is essential to check her carefully for perhaps two weeks before her heat period is due to accurately determine day 1 of the cycle.

The mating

Standard procedure

You will probably be required to take your bitch to the stud dog. This means that she will be going into strange territory and she may wish to check it out first, moving around the yard reading the smells. If the dog is free in the yard he will probably follow her around, sniffing her hindquarters and attempting to gain her attention. If you can see that the bitch is attempting to 'empty out' (relieve herself), it is preferable to restrain the dog to allow her to do this without interference.

Courtship
This takes various forms but usually the dog and bitch face each other, sniffing, with tails raised high. The bitch may flirt with the dog—pounce towards him or even on him and turn her rear end towards his head. It is also not unusual for the bitch to mount the dog during courtship. During this time a good stud dog will 'play' with the bitch, licking her vulva and attempting to gain her acceptance.

A sure sign with some stud dogs that a bitch is ready to be mated is that his teeth begin to 'chatter' (click together).

Standing
Eventually the dog will begin to attempt to mount the bitch, usually proceeding from the side and making his way to the back of her while grasping her across the back with his front legs. At this stage the bitch should stand, that is, should hold herself firmly and swing her tail to the side to allow penetration. During this stage the maiden bitch may need support from her owner, depending on her nature. Usually all that is required is to hold her head and talk to her reassuringly.

Copulation
It is not unusual for a dog to mount, thrust and dismount several times before actually penetrating the vagina with his penis. At this point the muscles of the vagina will contract around the penis and a tie will occur.

The tie
When the dog's penis is implanted in the vagina, the bulb of the penis enlarges and the dog begins to release spermatozoa into the area around the cervix. Usually

during this period the dog will slip to the side of the bitch, taking one of his back legs over her back, and the animals will end up rear-to-rear in the position known as the tie. They remain in this position until the ejaculation is complete. This is usually around 15 minutes but may last from 5 to 40 minutes with equally satisfactory results, as the maximum amount of sperm is pumped into the bitch within the first 3 to 5 minutes. It is essential during the tie to remain with the animals, probably holding the bitch from the front or supporting her from under the body. Apart from reassuring the bitch, it is also necessary not to allow her to lie down or attempt to roll over as this can cause injury to the dog. It is, however, quite common for the animals to move around in the tied position.

At the conclusion of the tie the animals will move apart. They may require a drink of water and will probably be quite tired and content to rest.

It is possible for puppies to ensue from a slip-mating. This occurs when the dog penetrates and ejaculates, even briefly, but does not tie.

The second mating

It is common among breeders to offer a second mating 36 hours after the first. This is to maximise the chance of achieving the mating at the correct period of ovulation and thus maimise the chances of fertilisation occurring. With an untried bitch it is probably advisable, keeping in mind that it may result in a larger litter. Experienced breeders who are confident of knowing the correct time for the mating often prefer not to do the second mating.

Variations from the norm

So far we have been considering a standard mating procedure, without any complications. In fact the Border Collie is known to be fairly trouble-free as far as mating and whelping are concerned, and it is the responsibility of every Border Collie breeder to make sure this continues to be the case by not breeding animals with breeding or whelping problems, as the causes of these are usually inheritable. The minor problems which a novice breeder may encounter include:

1. A very aggressive or frightened bitch may attempt to bite the dog, especially as he begins penetration. This should not be allowed to happen and the bitch may need to be muzzled or to be controlled by a very experienced and strong pair of hands. In extreme cases the bitch may require calming down using some form of sedative; however, this should only be done under the supervision of a vet. (I once had occasion to use my stud dog over another breeder's bitch and as the bitch was known to be extremely difficult to mate we took the precaution of giving her a sedative. I believe our timing was impeccable as very shortly after the tie occurred the bitch dozed off to sleep with her front legs on the floor and her hindquarters raised, firmly locked to the dog. To his credit, the dog was very patient about it all!)

2. Either the dog or the bitch may resent human interference. When the dog begins to mount he may dismount as soon as the handler attempts to hold the bitch. The bitch on the other hand may show confusion, attempting to gain the owner's attention in between flirting with the stud dog. If the dog is known to be a reliable stud dog and the bitch appears to be quite accepting of the proceedings, then allow them their privacy—but keep an eye on them as it is important to be in contact with them as soon as the tie takes place. Obviously to do this requires that the mating take place in a confined area. I had occasion to take two different bitches of mine to a particular stud dog; on each occasion the dog showed no interest until his owner and I moved out of sight and then he 'enticed' the bitch to the rear of a shed and had her tied in a very short time! On another occasion, following an unsuccessful hour with a stud dog in his backyard, his owner (an old friend) suggested I borrow the dog for a couple of days. I unthinkingly put them together in the back of my station wagon (a very confined space). I had barely driven four or five kilometres when I glanced in the rearvision mirror and was amazed to see the animals in a tie! I pulled over until the mating was completed and then returned the dog to his owner!

3. Sometimes the bitch appears willing but the dog sniffs and walks away. No amount of enticing can get him to do his job. This is very frustrating for the owners of both animals, but usually indicates either that the bitch is not yet ready to be mated, or that she has a problem such as an infection which would prevent a fruitful mating taking place.

I firmly believe, and have experienced this many times with my own stud dog, that a good stud dog can sense (or smell) when a mating would simply be a waste of time and effort on his part, and he will not bother. Do not mistake this for laziness or indifference on the part of the dog. Of course, there are very aggressive stud dogs who will still mate a bitch under these circumstances, usually with little effect.

4. The aged, arthritic or overweight dog. As already

stated it is preferable to put a maiden bitch to a proven stud dog. As far as possible the dog should be reasonably young and active. However, the occasion may arise where a breeder wishes to use a particular stud dog (perhaps to gain a bloodline). If the dog is old, or suffering from obesity or arthritis, then special assistance may be necessary.

The stud master

There may be occasions when either the bitch or the dog needs assistance to effect a mating and breeders may then require the services of a stud master. The stud master is usually a very experienced dog-handler who has a way with dogs and who has, with much experience, developed a knack of determining the problem and taking steps to correct it. Some of the difficulties which may benefit from the services of the stud master are: old or overweight dogs having difficulty mounting and penetrating, dogs with arthritis, fear-biting bitches, dogs of incompatible size, maiden dogs or bitches. A fee is usually involved for the services of the Stud Master.

The stud dog

The average breeding bitch may produce between six to ten litters in her lifetime—an average of fifty to sixty puppies over twelve to fourteen years. A stud dog, on the other hand, may very well average fifty puppies in six months. It becomes quite obvious that few stud dogs are warranted to service the available bitches. So breeders can be very selective in their choice of a 'good' stud dog.

I am quite regularly asked by owners of male Border Collies for advice on getting their dog used at stud. It should be understood that without some success in the show or trial ring or some very special quality or bloodline to offer the breed, an unknown dog has very little chance of obtaining stud work. The only sure way to turn a dog into a 'stud dog' is to buy yourself a bitch!

What makes a good stud dog?

1. In assessing a dog's potential as a sire it is necessary to look past the dog himself and to look closely at his offspring.

Is he passing on to his progeny some or all of the desirable and essential qualities of the Border Collie? Is he in some way improving the breed? Are his progeny at least equal to or better than their sire and dam?

2. It is more often likely that a stud dog will improve on his progeny in some areas but not in all. He can still be a good stud dog, if used to bitches which complement his weaknesses. The onus is on the owner of the dog to recognise his dog's strong and weak attributes and to be prepared to discuss them with the owners of potential mates.

3. A good stud dog should be virile and active and able to successfully execute a mating without interference.

4. A stud dog should not pass on to his offspring any heritable defects known to adversely affect the breed.

It is well to note here that a good stud dog or for that matter a good brood bitch need not necessarily be show champions themselves. It is well known that many show champions have been the offspring of mediocre parents. What is more important to consider is the genetic background of the dog. (See Chapter 6.)

As a general rule breeders prefer not to use their dogs at stud before they are approximately one year old. However, they can continue to be used while they are capable of producing fertile semen—usually with a Border Collie until the age of twelve or even older in some cases. With the older stud dog it may be necessary to have an occasional sperm count performed by your vet. Probably the main problem encountered with an older stud dog would be difficulties in mounting or holding the bitch because of obesity or arthritis in which case, some assistance may be necessary.

How often should a dog be allowed to be used at stud?

It is very unlikely that stud appointments would come so close together as to reduce the dog's ability to perform. In fact, if the dog is capable, matings could take place in close succession as sperm is produced during the mating. More pertinent considerations are:

1. Is your dog improving the breed sufficiently to warrant being used over a wide range of bitches?

2. Do you wish your bloodlines to be widely disseminated?

3. Is the market over-supplied with puppies? Alternatively, is the mating being undertaken for any particular reason other than to sell puppies?

Condition and general well being

The effect that stud work has on dogs varies with the individual. To begin with, breeders and show dog owners believe it is advisable (even desirable) to allow a young dog a mating before he reaches the age of about eighteen months, as this tends to cause the dog to mature, shown in the manner of his chest development, stance and general demeanour around other dogs. (However, if there is any possibility of CL (see page 95) the dog should not be used at stud before the age of two years.)

For some dogs subsequent matings have little further effect, while for others continuous stud work causes them to lose condition so that even their coat begins to look poorly. Simply having a bitch in season close enough for a dog to pick up her scent can have a similar effect. Some dogs respond to this by showing signs of fretfulness and loss of appetite and thus drop condition. When a dog is required to be in good show condition then sometimes it is preferable to delay his stud work.

Stud fee

The stud fee is usually assessed relative to the price of puppies. It is reasonable to assume that a titled dog (championship or obedience title, depending upon the requirements of the breeder), known to be throwing good quality puppies, will command a higher fee than an unproven or untitled dog. It is not uncommon to ask for a puppy in lieu of a stud fee.

The terms

To enable the registration of the litter a Service Certificate must be completed by both the owner of the dog and the owner of the bitch. This is usually signed by the owner of the stud dog on the day of mating and kept by the owner of the bitch until the litter is born. At that stage it is completed with details of the whelps and returned to the appropriate Kennel Control body. The forms are obtained from the Kennel Control body.

The terms for the mating are negotiated between the owner of the dog and the owner of the bitch. As already mentioned this is usually the current market price of a puppy or the stud dog owner's choice of 'pick of the litter'. This means exactly what it says. If the two owners agree to the mating on the basis of 'pick of the litter', the owner of the dog is entitled to first choice of any pup from the litter. (It is too late then to change the

terms, though you may see an especially outstanding pup that you want to keep for yourself.) When arranging a mating discuss with the stud dog's owner the procedure if no puppies ensue from the mating (which is not uncommon in maiden bitches). Usually, a return mating is offered when the bitch comes back into season.

Gestation period

Gestation period refers to the period of time from the date of fertilisation of the ova to the birth of the puppies—mating to whelping—a period of sixty-three days. Again you are advised to mark down the date on which the mating took place and the date by which all should be in readiness for the whelping.

Bitches are usually very reliable but it is not uncommon for the birth to be a day or two early or up to four days late. For the first six weeks of gestation the bitch should be treated as normal. She should be fed the same diet as she has been receiving so far but with the addition of a calcium supplement to ensure good bone development. The calcium may be in powdered or tablet form and therefore should be given according to the directions.

It is important not to over-feed the bitch during this period as obesity can lead to whelping problems. She should also be kept well exercised. This should not be a matter of chance but the owner should ensure that she is at least walked adequately each day. Again, a fit healthy bitch in good muscle tone will whelp with less trouble. Throughout the pregnancy the bitch should be bathed and brushed as normal. Toenails should be kept clipped and matted dead coat stripped regularly. The bitch will feel better and of course she will enjoy the contact with her owner. During the week before the due date of the whelping you may wish to clip the long hair around the vulva, to make it a little easier to keep her clean during the whelping. During this week the bitch's belly can be given a good wash, gently of course, and the nipples massaged with a little oil, e.g. olive oil, to keep them supple. From week six onwards begin to increase the bitch's rations of nutritional food, e.g. meat, egg yolk, adding a vitamin supplement and a milk substitute such as Denkavit to assist lactation. The bitch will become extremely hungry at this stage and by approximately week eight should be receiving about double her normal food intake. When the bitch is close to whelping, perhaps 24 hours away, she may refuse to eat at all. This is quite normal and she should not be forced in any way.

Discharge

Check your bitch at weekly intervals throughout her gestation period. If you can see any signs of a discharge from the vulva, particularly if it is dark in colour (greenish) and offensive in smell, you need to take her to the vet as this is usually a sign of uterine infection. As the whelping date approaches the bitch may show a pink or clear discharge which is normal.

Signs of pregnancy

A most common question, especially with breeders expecting their first litter is, 'Can you tell if my bitch is having puppies?' My answer is always, 'No,' but I can check to see if she is showing signs of a possible whelping! The only positive way to determine whether or not a bitch is pregnant is to have her x-rayed after about the seventh week of pregnancy. Unless there are other reasons to do this, with only two weeks to go it is not recommended. The only other possible time to check for developing embryos is between days twenty-one and twenty-five of the pregnancy when very experienced and skilled hands may be able to 'feel' marble-shaped 'lumps' at intervals along the Fallopian tubes by palpating the abdominal wall. I must stress that this requires very gentle, careful handling to avoid damage to the developing puppies and therefore should only be done by someone with the necessary experience. There are, however, some external signs to watch for, which may indicate that the bitch is in whelp:
• The vulva does not return to its normal size but remains soft and enlarged.
• The bitch may seek increased attention from her owner, described by breeders as 'acting sooky' or 'acting different'.
• As the pregnancy progresses the bitch may appear quieter than normal, perhaps taking more naps.
• The bitch may appear ravenous and go looking for food.
• The mammary glands begin to develop, commonly appearing as a faint blue circle around the nipple. Sometimes during the last two weeks of pregnancy it becomes possible to express milk from the nipples.
• Towards the latter part of the pregnancy the bitch may begin to take on a pear-shaped appearance. At this stage you may notice her having difficulty sitting or lying comfortably and 'when she walks, she waddles', so to speak!
• Finally, late in her gestation period, she will probably begin to dig holes in various places or scratch around more intensely.

These are generalised indications only, and signs vary from bitch to bitch.

False or phantom pregnancy

It is not uncommon, especially in maiden bitches, for a bitch to have a 'phantom' pregnancy. Due to an imbalance in hormone levels a bitch, having been mated, may show signs of gestation, even to the point of excreting milk, and may not be pregnant. This is disappointing to the new breeder, but not uncommon. The bitch will return to normal after the supposed whelping date; no special treatment is required if a normal pregnancy results from the next heat-period mating.

Preparing for whelping

If left without interference, the Border Collie bitch would do all the necessary work to prepare for her own whelping. That is to say, she would find a suitable dry sheltered area, perhaps under a tree or shed, dig a hole and make a nest. You can be sure her nest would be the ideal place for her to drop her litter and keep them warm and dry and nourished. However, as breeders we choose to make all the arrangements on behalf of our charges, but according to our requirements and not the bitch's. I am convinced that what we offer for the whelping and raising of a litter is not as appropriate as a Border Collie bitch provides for herself.

Despite the bitch's capabilities and because we like to feel that we are doing the right thing, breeders usually prepare whelping quarters as follows:

1. A warm, sheltered area reasonably close to your place of normal activity. This may be a back verandah or laundry area, for example, accessible for you to keep an eye on the bitch during the six to twenty hours of whelping.

2. A whelping box. This provides the bitch with a confined area in which she can prepare her nest. It is wise to have the whelping box prepared several weeks in advance and to encourage the bitch to sleep in it during the latter stages of the pregnancy. Thus she can be encouraged to scratch up old newspapers in the whelping box provided for that purpose.

3. A supply of old clean newspapers. Several layers of newspaper are used to line the floor of the whelping box. As her time approaches the bitch will tear and scratch them into a sizeable mound. This will provide the puppies with a soft landing and a place of warmth and concealment as the whelping goes on. Don't underestimate the amount of newspaper required, as the scratching and tearing may start several days early. Also, after the whelping, fresh paper is required for the bitch and the puppies to sleep on for some weeks.

A word of caution on the use of blankets, sheeting or sacking—the bitch will claw and scratch, causing tears and loose threads to appear. As the puppies wriggle around, small toenails, heads and even whole puppies can get caught up in rips and loose threads, causing distress and sometimes danger. Clean newspaper is known to be hygienic and when soiled can be simply burned and replaced with a fresh supply.

4. Heating: Commonsense is required here. Border Collies are working dogs and therefore are relatively hardy. Furthermore, if your bitch is the type that has a good thick coat and dense undercoat she can become overheated. (Whelping is quite an active process!) Therefore if the area is warm, dry and sheltered and the temperature mild, extra heating is probably not required.

If the weather is extremely or unusually cold some supplementary heating may be necessary. This should be kept warm, not hot. Take care to use a safe form of heating, especially if you intend to leave the bitch and pups unattended for long periods. (Small or ailing pups may require additional warmth—see page 37.)

5. Light: In most cases bitches begin to whelp just on dusk and continue on through the night (nature's way of ensuring survival). I have found a bedlamp will give sufficient light for you to follow proceedings while not disturbing the bitch as much as a full-on light would do.

6. Optional items:
• Notebook, pen and scales. Many breeders like to keep a record of the order in which the puppies are born, their sex and weight.
• Several old towels, hotwater bottle, cardboard box or clothes basket, scissors. (These may, but hopefully, won't be, used—see page 37.)
• Sustenance for owner (coffee/tea).

The pre-whelp week

With five to seven days to go, the pregnant bitch should be 'bulging at the sides' and slowing down in her movements. Allow her to rest as much as she wishes, preferably in the area in which the whelping is to take place. Encourage her to sleep in or close to the whelping box. As she begins to nest, direct her into the whelping box.
• Bathing: If you feel it is necessary and if you have convenient facilities, the bitch may be given a bath a week or so before whelping is due. Of course, this must be done with care and gentleness. Do not attempt to lift her at this time nor to manoeuvre her in too small a space. She should be towelled thoroughly and kept warm until her thick coat is completely dry to the skin; if she is accustomed to it, use a hairdryer.
• Clipping: You may wish to trim the hair around the vulva for convenience of cleaning.
• Nails: Check and trim if necessary.
• Nipples: Clean and massage wth oil.
• Medication: In line with your vet's advice you may have to begin giving your bitch antibiotic tablets. (See section on 'fading' puppies, page 38.)
• Temperature: Check the bitch's temperature at about day 58. (See below.)

Whelping

Signs of imminent whelping

Following is a list of indications that the bitch is within 24 hours of whelping. (Remember that this may occur 2 or 3 days earlier than the specified 63 days.) It is preferable that the bitch's owner stays accessible to her. If this is not possible then try to arrange a replacement, someone with whom the bitch is familiar and friendly and ideally an experienced dog person.

1. The body temperature drops 1–2 degrees, i.e. from a norm of between 37.5° to 38.8°C to approximately 36°C.

2. The bitch feels cold and clammy to touch and begins to twitch intermittently.

3. Restlessness, agitation and stress signs become more obvious.

4. Nesting becomes more vigorous, almost frantic.

5. The bitch may refuse to eat. This is a guide only.

I have known a particularly greedy bitch to eat a meal two hours before whelping, only to vomit it when whelping began.

6. Puffing and panting begins. By this time of course, the bitch should be confined to her whelping box with a familiar face checking her regularly and giving her reassurance and comfort. Water should be available.

7. Involuntary labour begins—noticed as muscular movements in the area of the flanks. The time intervals vary and involuntary labour may last as little as an hour or up to four hours. As voluntary labour draws closer the muscle movement increases in intensity and frequency.

8. Voluntary labour begins—at this stage the bitch will begin to stand and crouch (this position appears similar to that adopted for defaecation). The bitch will strain and push in an attempt to expel the whelp. The time period during voluntary labour varies; the bitch may drop her puppies as close together as ten minutes apart or as far apart as two hours. Often, after the first puppy, the bitch will rest for perhaps thirty to sixty minutes before beginning again.

(*Note:* Two-hourly intervals between puppies is not uncommon. However, a longer period than this, especially if the bitch appears distressed or in pain, may indicate birth difficulties and the bitch may require veterinary assistance.)

The arrival of the puppies

Generally, as each puppy is born it is still enclosed in the sac or placental membrane and attached to the umbilical cord. The bitch will bite through the sac, eating it as she goes, and similarly will chew through the cord, often continuing to gnaw at it until it is quite short. She will then begin to 'work' on the puppy, licking it and moving it around, often frantically, to stimulate breathing. The puppy will then be licked clean and dry.

Throughout this process, provided there are no complications, there should be no interference from persons supervising the whelping. Once the puppy is moving and breathing the bitch will usually begin activities in the area of the vulva, expelling and eating the afterbirth and licking herself clean. She may then rest up and encourage the new puppy to suckle while waiting for the next delivery.

The time interval between puppies varies but if voluntary labour goes beyond two hours, with obvious signs of distress and straining, assistance should be sought. As a rough guide a bitch showing signs of involuntary labour at around dusk and producing her first puppy by about 9 pm will usually complete an average whelping of seven or eight puppies by 2 or 3 am.

Anxiety

Throughout the whelping it is best to disturb the bitch as little as possible, as many become extremely anxious. During this time the newspaper may become a bloody sodden mess, but any attempt to replace it and clean up before the bitch is finished will probably cause her to fret and fuss and attempt to get the soiled paper back into the whelping box. Breeders will sometimes try to remove puppies to a box while each drop is in progress for fear of the bitch accidentally standing on or injuring those already born. You will know by the bitch's reaction whether to take this precaution or not. I have seen bitches so anxious about their puppies that they will 'hold back' and even leave the whelping box searching for and trying to retrieve the puppies that have been removed. This behaviour, of course, is quite normal and instinctive and stems from their great urge to protect, raise and regenerate the species.

Though the bitch may appear to be scratching, circling and straining in a frenzy, she is usually quite adept at avoiding the other puppies in the whelping box. Occasionally you may get a 'rough' bitch or if the litter is quite large in number it may be necessary to remove some of the puppies to safety. The most practical way to do this is to have a small cardboard box in readiness. Half fill a hotwater bottle with hot (not boiling) water, place it in the cardboard box and cover it with a folded towel or similar. Put the puppies on top of the towel and place another towel loosely over the top of them, covering them completely. A number of different approaches may have to be tried here. If you leave one or two puppies with the bitch and remove the remainder you may get away with it! Or you could try leaving the cardboard box with the pups in it in the whelping box. (My experience with this is that the bitch will remove the puppies as fast as you can put them in or will try to get into the cardboard box herself!) I recall an old brood bitch of mine, one known as a 'real good mum', having a litter of nine puppies. It became obvious to me as the whelping proceeded that the puppies were quite ill. In an attempt to keep them warm until I could get medical help I loaded them into my cane washing basket complete with towels and hotwater bottle. Unfortunately seven of the puppies died and the bitch was left with two to raise. For several weeks afterwards, whenever she saw that clothes basket, even if I was carrying it full of wet clothes, she made frantic attempts to get into it and scratch around in it, obviously looking for her pups. By and large a bitch is more accepting and less disturbed by puppies that die while in her care than by puppies being taken away while still alive.

Once you are sure that the whelping is complete, it may be appropriate to put the puppies into a warm box and take the bitch outside, on a lead if necessary, to relieve herself. While this is happening the whelping box could be cleaned up, all the soiled newspaper removed and burnt or disposed of and several layers of fresh paper put down. Return the puppies to the box, and let the bitch settle down to feed the puppies undisturbed.

How will you know when the whelping is complete?

This is a question for which there is no sure answer. The best guide is the bitch herself. As a general rule, she will know when she has delivered all of her puppies and will convey this to you by her relaxed manner, by her desire to rest and perhaps to eat and drink. An experienced breeder is usually able to read the signs from the appearance of the bitch, but sometimes the bitch has the last laugh. With my very first litter, having prepared myself beforehand, I thought I knew when my bitch had finished whelping. She had four pups, had willingly gone outside to relieve herself, even eaten a bowl of mush I offered her and then settled down to allow the pups to feed. As it had been two hours since her last pup and no further straining was taking place I decided she had finished and went to bed. I felt quite satisfied with my first effort, though a little disappointed at the size of the litter. When I went into the laundry to check her out the next morning she had eight beautiful pups! I swear she looked at me as if to say 'Fooled you!'

The only sure way to know if a bitch has completed her labour is to have her checked by a vet. With a normal whelping this is not absolutely necessary, but if she continues to strain or appears to have contractions with nothing resulting or appears stressed or agitated for a period of approximately two hours, then call in a vet.

The whelping completed

Once she has delivered all of her puppies, provided the delivery has been normal and without problems, the bitch will show signs of relaxation. She may be prepared to accept a drink of warm milk and glucose (though she will probably not want to eat at this stage) and may even make a very quick trip to outside to relieve herself. Most bitches lick themselves and their puppies quite clean, then stretch full length to allow the puppies to suckle. At this stage the bitch quite often naps, looking tired but content, and is happy to accept some patting and sweet talk from her owner. She's been very clever and she knows it!

Eating the afterbirth

Many dog owners, especially those going through their first whelping, become very distressed when seeing the bitch devour the afterbirth. They then try to remove each placenta before the bitch can get to them. My advice, if asked about this, is—don't! I firmly believe that where the bitch is concerned her survival instincts are usually the best guide. The eating of the afterbirth is part of the instinctive cleaning up process which was necessary in the wild to reduce the possibility of predators picking up the scent of the litter. However, studies indicate that it is also beneficial to the bitch, being a source of nutrition and a link in the release of the hormones which are part of the complete process of whelping. If the real reason that people try to stop the bitch from eating the afterbirth is because it upsets them to see her do it, the solution is obvious—don't watch!

Eating dead whelp

Though not a common or pleasant occurrence a whelp born dead or dying soon after whelping is sometimes eaten by the bitch. Though distasteful to witness, this action must be kept in perspective, that is, as an instinctive response to generations of conditioning. The bitch has not suddenly become cannibalistic or vicious but is probably cleaning up to remove the possibility of a decomposing, smelly carcass attracting predators. Through this action she is really protecting her live offspring.

Appearance of the puppies

To the uninitiated the newborn Border Collie may be different to what was expected; it is usually described as otter-like. (See photo on page 33.) The coat is sleek and smooth against the body and the tail is almost rat-like. Perhaps the head causes the most surprise as it is often quite large in proportion to the rest of the body, with a very squashed-in appearance to the rest of the face. The muzzle appears very pink as nose and lip pigment is often not present at birth, the eyes are closed and the ears are usually flattened against the head and pointing upwards.

Markings are usually well defined at this stage though occasionally some extra fine white hairs will occur along the ear pinna (lobe edge); they usually grow out as the ear feathering develops. Some pups have an extended white blaze over the top of the head which almost closes over as the head broadens and develops. Small body-coloured spots on the muzzle and legs are rarely discernible at birth, but appear at around four to six weeks of age. (Ticking is discussed in Chapter 6.)

Colour
The main coat colour will appear and develop as follows:
• Black: Black at birth, varying in the adult dog between jet black, smokey black and rusty black.
• Chocolate: Deep to medium brown at birth, may lighten to tan or rust shades.
• Blue: May range from steel grey, blue grey to smokey black at birth; almost always darkens. Sometimes the adult dog becomes indiscernible from a dusty black.
• Red: Almost white or very light cream at birth, darkens to fawn, wheaten or ginger with maturity.
• Tri-colour: Often very difficult to pick at birth, appearing black and white; the tan markings may first be seen under the tail as a pale lemon; after two or three days the tan spots above the eyebrows may be noticed; the tan markings darken in the adult dog.

Sex
It is a relatively simple matter to determine a puppy's gender.

Place puppy carefully on its back and examine beneath its tail and along its belly. The bitch will have two apertures, the anus immediately below the tail set, followed closely by the vulva. The dog will have the anus only and then along the mid-line towards the umbilical cord the encased penis will be found. It is very unlikely that you will be able to see the testes at this stage of development of the puppy. Your vet should check for the presence of testes in the puppy at six weeks of age.

Dewclaws
These are one of the digits reduced in size (equivalent to our thumb or big toe) complete with a nail, sometimes found on the inside of the dog's limbs. Dewclaws are considerably less developed than the remaining four digits and in fact many Border Collies are born without dewclaws on their hind legs. Check puppies shortly after birth as dewclaws occurring on the hind legs are best removed (by a vet) at about the age of three days. Front limb dewclaws, however, are not removed.

Litter size
The number of pups in a litter can vary from as few as one to as many as eleven; very rarely more (though both these extremes would be quite unusual). In the main a Border Collie produces seven or eight puppies per litter.

Puppies from birth to eight weeks

With the whelping completed very little is required of the breeder insofar as the care of the puppies is concerned. The bitch will adequately care for the puppies provided she herself is well nourished and has a good milk supply and provided that the litter is average sized and healthy. (Specific problems are treated on pages 37–38.)

Feeding
Stimulated by the dam and responding with instinctive reflex actions puppies will find their way to and onto the nipples of the bitch's mammary glands, sucking vigorously until full and then will simply fall asleep.

Occasionally puppies will have difficulty sucking because of the bitch having small or inverted nipples. This condition may be helped by gently massaging the nipple, rolling it between thumb and forefinger, and helping the puppies to take it and begin sucking. Usually the problem corrects itself once the puppies are able to suck srongly and hold on.

It is important that all puppies suckle from the bitch during the first three days to ensure an intake of colostrum. Colostrum is the highly nutritious milk produced by the bitch during the first three days after whelping; it contains important antibodies which protect the puppies from viral or bacterial infection. These antibodies can only be absorbed by the puppies during the first three days of life, before their own digestive systems have developed.

Bowel and bladder functions

As puppies have no conscious control over their bowel and bladder functions until approximately three weeks of age, the task of 'emptying out' the puppies falls to the dam. She will lick them vigorously in the region of the anus and genitals and simply eat the resulting motions. In fact, even when reflex or conscious actions cause defaecation to occur, the bitch will still clean up after her offspring. Most Border Collie bitches keep the whelping box quite clean.

Warmth

As puppies under the age of one week are unable to regulate their own body temperature, being unable to shiver to get themselves warm, they must be kept warm to enable them to rest contentedly between feedings. Usually this task also falls to the bitch but circumstances may arise which require that additional heating be provided.

Normal contented full puppies will pile up close together or on top of one another and sleep soundly. Puppies which continuously roll around, squirm or whimper are giving signs of distress. One of the common problems of this is coldness. Other possible problems such as hunger or illness are discussed on pages 37–38.

General guide to puppies' progress

• The umbilical cord should have dried up and dropped off by about day four.
• Eyes open between days 10 to 14, but the ability to focus does not develop until approximately three to four weeks. The eye colour will at first appear to be blue, gradually darkening to brown by about eight weeks of age.
• Hearing—until the age of two weeks the puppies' ears are closed and they hear very little. By about three weeks, they should begin to respond to sounds.
• By three weeks of age the puppies are beginning attempts to walk, often falling down and rolling over, but quite quickly managing several 'struts' across the whelping box. Often by about week four the puppies are play-fighting with each other. Also at about this time the bitch will begin to stand to feed the puppies, forcing them to stretch upwards on their back legs. This encourages strong muscle development and balance.
• Milk-teeth, canines and incisors begin to erupt during the second or third week, often becoming a source of irritation to the bitch.
• Puppies should grow quite rapidly during this early period. To ensure a strong, healthy and full sized adult dog, it is suggested that the puppy double its body weight by 12 to 14 days. Weaning can begin between three to four weeks.
• Nails grow quite rapidly and can cause scratches on the dam's belly. They can be safely clipped.
• By about four weeks of age puppies have begun to outgrow the whelping box and may need to be moved to larger, safer quarters. At this stage they have begun socialisation and exploring activities.
• Between four and five weeks approximately, some puppies will be attempting to bark.
• From the third week onward the puppy enters its peak learning period.

Weaning

Puppies are usually introduced to solid food from the age of about three or four weeks, varying with circumstances. If the litter size is small, the bitch has plenty of milk and is still willing to feed them, and if the puppies appear to be doing well, then weaning can be delayed. On the other hand, with eight to nine puppies to feed the bitch may become sore and scratched and show signs of reluctance to remain with the pups; in this case weaning can begin at three weeks.

I usually begin weaning with the first feed of the day, separating the bitch and offering the puppies a bowl of very mushy cereal mixed with a diluted milk substitute. I find Weet-Bix nutritious and inexpensive and apparently quite appealing to the puppies' taste. Some breeders prefer to use a puppy cereal obtainable commercially.

A variety of milk substitutes are available, such as Denkavit and Animalac, and reduced milks such as Carnation. Cow's milk is best avoided as it is higher in lactose than is desirable and tends to cause looseness in young puppies. The main thing to remember is to dilute any milk to about half strength to begin with gradually increasing the strength as the puppies' digestive systems become accustomed to the change in diet. To this mixture I like to add some powdered glucose and egg yolk and later some powdered calcium carbonate.

Standing to feed
signals the onset
of weaning

Teaching puppies to eat

Use a large, shallow container, perhaps a round tray with 2.5–4 cm high sides and fill it with the cereal mixture. Some of the puppies will stumble into the dish and begin sucking or licking. Others will need to be gently 'nosed' into the dish—perhaps put a little of the mixture onto your finger and into the puppy's mouth. On their first attempt puppies usually get more food on themselves than in their mouths, but they will lick it off themselves and each other, gradually recognising it as food.

After three or four days a second meal is introduced, perhaps mid-afternoon. I usually repeat the cereal but with a small quantity of minced beef mixed through. The puppies will usually eat this mixture with no trouble at all. Three to four days later vary one of the meals to include commercial puppy food, e.g. Harper's Puppy Chow or Lucky Puppy Mini, well soaked beforehand in warm water to soften. By about the beginning of week five, begin to offer the puppies a drink of milk or milk substitute at mid-day. Also by now they should be used to having a bowl of clean, fresh water in their pens at all times.

You should aim to have the puppies eating well and accustomed to a variety of foods and tastes by the time they are ready to be sold. A suggested menu to aim for by the end of week six would be as follows:

Breakfast—cereal, milk substitute, egg yolks, glucose and calcium

Mid-day—soaked puppy kibble (complete dog food variety), e.g. Harper's Puppy Chow

Mid-afternoon—milk substitute to drink

Evening meal—meat and kibble mix with a vitamin supplement added, e.g. Petvite

At the same time as the puppies are being weaned, the bitch is drying up her milk supply. If possible arrange the puppy pen so that the bitch can take herself away from the pups for rest periods. By about the fourth week the bitch will have started to stand to allow the puppies to suckle, encouraging them to stretch and balance and exercise their hindquarters. She will leave them for longer periods of time. Often her belly will be quite red and scratched and this will usually signal to her to begin leaving her pups for increased periods of time. One way of allowing the bitch to leave the puppy pen is to place a sturdy box, bench or table in the pen, low enough for her to jump onto but high enough to prevent the puppies following.

A soothing non-toxic cream, e.g. anhydrous lanolin or olive oil, may be rubbed onto the bitch's belly to give her some relief from her soreness.

Socialisation

Between three and twelve weeks a puppy's brain is most receptive to learning and conditioning; during play with its litter mates each puppy is becoming aware of and developing its survival skills—climbing, pouncing, chewing, fighting and, for the Border Collie, crouching, setting and sometimes 'eyeing'. It is very important that the puppies receive human contact during this period. They should be picked up, handled, carried, nursed and petted. This will enable the puppies to be imprinted with positive associations—studies have shown that these associations mould the type of adult dog a puppy will grow into. Handling should always be gentle and should not hurt a puppy—no pushing or hitting! Puppies which are not socialised during this critical period or which are mistreated often have adjustment problems in adulthood, becoming timid, aggressive or difficult to train.

Worming

It should be appreciated that the presence of parasitic worms in puppies is inevitable, despite all precautions taken with the bitch and in the kennels. It is recommended that puppies be treated at 2, 4, 6 and 8 weeks of age and thereafter at monthly intervals until the age of six months. (Most recommendations involve a single dose wormer, but may vary with the treatment used.) The first two treatments may be given in syrup form and with an eyedropper can effectively be administered directly into the mouth. As the puppy grows in size and weight a tablet may be easier and more efficient. This could be given enclosed in some raw meat or pushed directly down the pup's throat. Some care is required here as puppies can spit out a tablet; as well, some vomit back the medication, thus rendering the treatment ineffective. (It can be very frustrating, having just wormed seven puppies, to suddenly find one tablet on the floor!) When a puppy is infested with worms it does not do well, losing much of the nutrition it requires for healthy development. The signs of worm infested puppies are:
• Anaemia (pale, poor looking gums)
• Lack of condition, though the stomach may have a bloated appearance
• Listlessness and lack of energy
• Loose motions (in severe cases blood is passed)
• Lack of sparkle to coat and eyes

Eating the droppings (coprophagy)

You may see puppies (and adult dogs) eating their own or other pups' faecal droppings. As I see it, there are two possible reasons for this: something lacking in the animal's diet or boredom. Coprophagy will cause the animal no real harm except where the droppings are a potential source of worm infestation. However, it is unacceptable behaviour for several reasons:

1. It indicates an underlying problem which should be dealt with and corrected, i.e. dietary deficiency or boredom.
2. It causes the puppy to have an unpleasant smell or breath which reduces the potential for loving and handling which a puppy should be receiving.
3. If left unchecked, coprophagy develops into a hard-to-break habit in the adult dog.

Small puppies should not be smacked or reprimanded for eating droppings, rather the underlying problem should be dealt with. Check the pup's diet. Make sure that it is receiving its essential food requirements and particularly that it is receiving enough bulk food to give it a 'full' feeling. If you are satisfied that the pup is well fed and healthy then check for the more common cause of coprophagy—boredom. Remember that puppies are inquisitive, energetic and social beings. They need stimulation and an occasional achievable challenge. Often it is necessary to keep puppies in a run or enclosed area but this can be made more interesting by the inclusion of balls, tin cans, boxes (to climb on and into), leather straps or other chewable objects. Clean up the puppy pen as often as possible, removing droppings two or three times daily both to reduce the temptation to eat them and for reasons of hygiene, lessening the risks of worm infestations.

Immunisations and vaccinations

As the time grows closer to when the puppies are to go to their new homes, reputable breeders will make arrangements to take the litter to a vet for an overall check and vaccinations. The vet should check each puppy thoroughly, indicating any problems which may be encountered, the presence of testes in males, problem bites, etc.

The ongoing vaccination program varies between different vets but in most cases an initial vaccination is given to cover canine distemper and measles, canine parvovirus and kennel cough if desired. Your vet should provide you with a vaccination certificate giving details of the vaccine used and suggested dates by which booster shots should be given. It is essential to pass this certificate on to the puppy's new owners and to explain to them that the first 'shot' the puppy has received does not give it permanent immunity.

Although there is quite a considerable cost involved in having a litter of puppies vaccinated I believe it is in the best interests of both the breeder and the puppies.

Bitch within hours of whelping a litter of nine

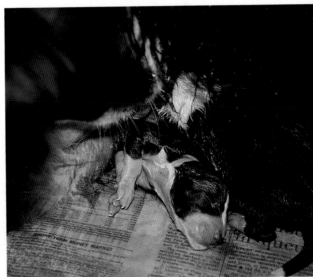

Whelping begins—the bitch is chewing through the foetal membrane as the puppy emerges

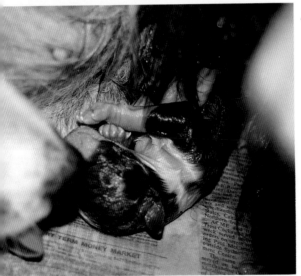

The bitch licks and moves the puppy vigorously to stimulate breathing

While the bitch is busy with the next whelp the others are active and looking for food, within quite a short time of being whelped

The bitch lifts a puppy with her mouth to bring it closer to her

With five on the ground and four to come the bitch is taking a well-earned rest. At birth these puppies weighed between 280 and 320 g

A puppy within minutes of birth

Five day old puppies, sleek and healthy, snuggling up to mum

The breeder will build up a reputation for selling healthy, well cared for puppies and the puppies stand a better chance of survival.

Heartworm
Puppies can commence heartworm treatment from the age of ten weeks, but it is essential that the puppy be checked for the presence of microfilariae before treatment is commenced.

Fundamentals of selling a registered litter

1. Owners of both sire and dam must be current members of a state canine control body.
2. Complete the service certificate with chosen names and all necessary details and forward it to the Kennel Control with payment for the registration of your litter.
3. Have the puppies' temporary vaccinations done at six weeks of age.
4. Prepare the paper work; the new owners should be given:
• Pedigree certificate
• Feeding chart
• Vaccination certificate
• Registration certificate if appropriate
• Receipt (Mark on the receipt 'sold with papers' or 'sold without papers' as the case may be.)
5. Place advertisements if necessary in newspapers, club journals, etc.
6. When expecting potential puppy buyers ensure that the puppies are clean and smell fresh and that the puppy run has been cleaned and disinfected.
7. General considerations: As a courtesy, enquire of the new owners if they have food available for the new puppy. (You may wish to provide a small parcel of kibble, calcium and milk substitute.) Also, be aware that when strangers begin to arrive and handle the pups your bitch may become quite protective of her offspring. It is a wise precaution to keep the bitch separate at this time; if the potential buyers wish to see the dam bring her out on a lead. Try to arrange the puppies so that they can be prevented from jumping up at potential buyers (who don't usually come in old gear!). Finally, give your telephone number to people who buy pups from you as they may wish to check on something at a later date.

The bitch post-weaning

Once the puppies are weaned and beginning to move to their new homes it is time to start thinking about the bitch and assisting her to return to condition.

Return to oestrus cycle
Exact times vary but a bitch is generally expected to come back into season by the time the puppies would be around 16–20 weeks old, that is, when she would normally be due. It is best to begin checking your bitch daily.

The next mating
Unless there are exceptional circumstances it is usual to allow the bitch a rest period between matings, at least one and possibly two oestrus cycles.

Coat condition and general health
Carrying, whelping and raising an average sized litter puts quite a strain on a bitch's body. Approximately 8–12 weeks from whelping the bitch will begin to lose coat quite prolifically. Comb and brush her to remove all the dead and loose hair. In most cases this is a staggering amount; suddenly the bitch looks bald and tatty. She will probably also have lost weight and may have a caved-in appearance. It will take possibly 3–4 months for her coat to regain its length and bloom and for her mammary glands and belly area to tighten up. You may also notice the vulva tighten up and reduce in size. Suggested procedure to aid her return to normal is:
• Strip the coat, cut away any matted hair and give her a thorough bath, cleansing the surface of the skin.
• Check toenails and clip if necessary.
• Check teeth and ears and clean if necessary.
• Feed a nutritious diet including fresh meat, egg yolk and coat improver.
• For approximately six weeks after weaning allow a bitch up to 30% more than normal rations, perhaps feeding her this for breakfast. It may be unwise to continue for too long a period.
• Maintain a regular exercise program to improve muscle tone and condition.
• Re-establish training, play periods, stimulating and interesting outings.
• Massage her belly for two or three weeks using cream or oil.
• Worm the bitch at two and four weeks after whelping and again six weeks later, then return to a normal worming routine.

Problems with breeding and whelping

In the main Border Collies are sound, honest animals developed to work and therefore to require, in modern terms, 'little cost and minimum maintenance'. In the earlier pastoral days, animals which incurred injury or illness or showed signs of whelping problems were very rarely rushed to the vet but more often left to cope or shot! As a result, the fittest and most capable survived and the Border Collie is now known among the veterinary fraternity and breeders as basically a relatively easy breeder.

However, as may be expected with the increasing popularity of the Border Collie and with the increasing number of breeders, some recurring problems are beginning to be encountered.

Some problems occur often enough to warrant all serious and concerned breeders being aware of them. Some are the result of viruses and affect all breeds; others are congenital, i.e. the result of non-normal conditions occurring during gestation or whelping. A third group results from heritable factors and can therefore be kept in hand by careful breeding programs. This requires a high degree of honesty and responsibility among breeders to educate themselves and others to an awareness of the problems and their causes.

The bitch

During gestation

Any excessive bleeding or unusual discharge during pregnancy, especially if it is greenish-black and putrid or foul-smelling, is a sign of problems. It could indicate an infection, a dead whelp or an impending abortion. A vet must be consulted quickly.

During whelping

1. Size problems, when a bitch cannot expel a whelp. The signs to watch for are prolonged and excessive straining (longer than 1–½ hours). This condition may be caused by the bitch's pelvis being too small relative to the size of the pup or by a smaller than usual number of pups in a litter (one or two), allowing them to become excessively large during gestation.
Veterinary assistance is required.
2. Malpresentation, a pup which is not in the correct position for expulsion. Possible causes are a dead whelp

(which is obviously unable to turn), or two pups presenting too closely together. Again, the sign will be excessive straining to the point of fatigue.
Veterinary assistance is required.
3. Tiredness, fatigue: If a bitch labours for too long she may lack the energy and drive required to complete the whelping.

Fatigue may be brought on by prolonged straining as a result of 1 or 2 above or as a result of a bitch being overweight, old or generally in poor condition. If, after a period of rest, she simply 'gives up', then a Caesarian section operation may be required.
Veterinary assistance is required.
4. Uterine inertia—basically, the inability of the muscles of the uterus to respond to the hormonal releases which initiate contractions. The bitch simply does not strain or push.
Veterinary assistance is required.
5. Stuck whelp: Occasionally a puppy may appear stuck halfway out of the vulva. If the head is presented then give the bitch a further 5–7 minutes to rest between contractions and to continue with the birth. After this time it may be necessary to give her some assistance. Watch for the next contraction and, using a clean towel and while the contraction is in progress, gently ease the puppy downwards and back towards the bitch. If the puppy is in breech position the same procedure applies, except that the sac will have to be broken after the puppy emerges. Whenever possible allow the bitch to be in control of stimulating the puppy and severing the cord.

Post-whelping

1. Retained foetus or placenta: This occasionally occurs with a large litter. A pup or afterbirth may be retained high up in the uterine horn, where it is almost impossible to detect. The outcome of this is that the matter decomposes and causes the bitch to become agitated and restless and to continue to strain. Progressive signs may be a high temperature and a dark coloured, offensive discharge.
Veterinary assistance is required.
2. Metritis, infection and inflammation of the uterus. It may occur as either acute or chronic.
• Acute metritis occurs very quickly, usually following a retained placenta or foetus or an abortion. The signs will be several of the following:

A high temperature
Listlessness, depression, sunken eyes
Excessive thirst, vomiting, straining, continuing to nest, digging
A decrease in the milk flow

A foul smelling, offensive discharge
Veterinary assistance is required *urgently*.

• Chronic metritis is a long-standing low-grade infection which is usually present in the bitch all year round but which is not obviously noticeable when attempting to produce a litter. The outcome may be puppies aborted, born dead or dying soon after birth, and infertility in the bitch.

Veterinary treatment is required prior to a mating being attempted.

3. Mastitis: An infection in the mammary glands which normally shows up within two weeks of whelping. The bitch shows signs of stress, whimpering and panting with a high temperature. She will not want to eat and her mammary glands will feel hot, swollen and hard. This is an extremely painful condition and can result in the development of abscesses. It may also occur at any stage of lactation and weaning.

Veterinary assistance is required.

4. Eclampsia ('milk fever'): This results from a depletion of the calcium reserves in the bitch (for the production of milk) and may occur two weeks before whelping and any time up to the period of weaning. The signs are:

Anxiety—the bitch becomes highly excited
Panting, whining
Muscular spasms and staggering

Eventually the bitch falls down and usually lies stiffly with her legs extended and her eyes wide open and staring.

This is an extreme emergency and *urgent* veterinary attention is required.

The condition can usually be treated successfully but it should be noted that a predisposition to eclampsia is considered to be heritable.

It is possible to reduce the risk of eclampsia by providing the bitch with an adequate intake of calcium, phosphorus and vitamin C during her pregnancy.

The puppies

Within a very short time of being born, normal healthy puppies with the assistance of their mother will make their way to the bitch and begin suckling. The bitch will continue to fuss over them for quite some time, licking them, rolling them around and nibbling at the cord. After the whelping is completed the puppies should settle down to eat and sleep in a contented fashion. Their main requirements at this stage are food,

warmth and rest. Throughout the whole process it is preferable to interfere with the puppies as little as possible and to give the dam every opportunity of doing all that is required herself. Sometimes a bitch with her first litter may appear a little slow and unsure, but usually her instincts will prompt her in the right direction. Following is a brief guide to times when assistance becomes necessary.

Breaking the sac

If after a minute or so the bitch has not attempted to release the pup, the sac may be torn open with the finger and the membrane pulled back off the puppy. The cord should be severed to within 2.5 cm of the belly and the puppy stimulated into breathing. Rub puppy vigorously on the chest with a piece of towel, holding the head tilted downwards to facilitate the removal of fluid from the lungs. Return the puppy to the bitch as soon as possible.

Puppies showing signs of distress

Whimpering, excessive squirming and rolling around combined with a cold, wrinkled skin, bluish colour and obvious anxiety on the part of the bitch are signs that something is amiss. If left unchecked progressive signs that a puppy is close to death (which may occur very quickly in newborn puppies) are that the puppy feels cold and clammy to touch and becomes quieter and less active. The three main causes of this type of behaviour are:

Cold
Puppies are unable to maintain an adequate body temperature and need to be kept at approximately 38°C. Some additional heating may be required in certain circumstances, e.g. in sudden cold weather, in draughty whelping quarters or in the case of inadequate care by the bitch. Ensure that heating provided is safe (electric cords which are safe from chewing, fuel heaters which can't be knocked over).

Hunger
Check that the bitch has an adequate milk supply. Supplementary feeding may be necessary with very large litters or if the dam has been through an illness or trauma. It is preferable to obtain a formula and instructions for supplementary feeding from a vet but

in an emergency mix 2 parts of Carnation Milk (or similar evaporated unsweetened milk) and 1 part of warm water and feed 5–10 ml every 2 hours with an eyedropper. Note that day and night feeding is required.

Viral or bacterial infection

There are many different types and causes of infection; they may be contracted in the uterus or after birth and may be generalised or localised in a puppy. Puppies under three days old have very little resistance and few reserves to call on and if an infection is not treated quickly they appear to simply fade away and die—dubbed the 'fading puppy' syndrome. An exacerbating factor is the newborn puppy's inability to resist the cold, which means that often pneumonia results. The only possible action is fast veterinary treatment, *keeping the puppy warm* in the meantime.

A newborn puppy with an infection in the intestinal tract will variously arch the back then hunch towards the stomach, considered a recognisable first sign of the 'fading puppy' syndrome. If not treated immediately, these puppies die within twenty-four hours, often much sooner. The most common cause is BHS streptococcal infection.

Recognising the possibility of such an occurrence, pre-treatment is recommended in the form of swabbing the bitch to check for infection and a course of antibiotics at the appropriate time during her pregnancy, depending upon the advice of your vet.

It should be recognised that infections can be carried continuously by the bitch in the form of low-grade metritis or that the bacteria may be introduced from the environment. It is also possible that an infection could be transferred from the dog to the bitch during mating but this is considered far less likely to happen and therefore a negligible risk.

Hypothermia

Puppies which have become separated from their dam lose body heat very quickly and will eventually go into a torpor, even to the point of stiffness. Contrary to what may appear to be the case these puppies, though they look dead, can be revived by heating them through to raise their body temperature. This may be done by putting the puppy in an electrically controlled foot-warming slipper or on an electric pad or blanket. If none of these are available place puppy, well wrapped in a towel, on several layers of newspaper in a conventional oven turned on to the minimum setting. Leave the door open and watch the puppy carefully for 20–30 minutes for signs of movement. The puppy's position may need to be varied during that time. Additional stimulation may be given in the form of a drop of brandy on the tongue. Once the puppy shows signs of reviving, return it to the bitch, perhaps expressing a few drops of milk from the dam and smearing it around the puppy's mouth. In extreme cases of shock fluid therapy may be required to be given by a vet.

Rejection by the bitch

Occasionally it will happen that a bitch will continuously push away a live pup or not gather-in one partcular pup. On the surface, the pup often appears normal and active and willing to suck and this behaviour by the bitch is bewildering to the inexperienced breeder. My own personal experience with such situations has been that these rejected pups have had some form of defect or sickness which is not immediately apparent but which can obviously be sensed in some way by the bitch. (It is widely considered that bitches and dogs can smell such things as infections or something amiss.) In these circumstances a suggested course of action would be to try to return the puppy to the bitch as often as possible over the next 24 hours and try holding the puppy on a nipple to suck. If after 24 hours the bitch continues to reject the pup then you may wish to attempt hand-rearing or have the pup checked by a vet. Considerations to take into account include the size of the remaining litter, the cost of correcting any deformity and the state of the puppy market.

(*Note:* These remarks do not apply to puppies suffering from hypothermia which, when revived, are usually accepted by the bitch, and grow into normal healthy puppies.)

Congenital malformations

By and large Border Collies are a sound, healthy breed but in any area of breeding the unexpected can still occur. The following malformations, though not common, are still known to occur in Border pups:

Cleft palate	Cryptorchidism
Extreme undershot jaw	Kinked tail
Umbilical hernia	Malformed chest

Some of these conditions are known to be heritable and for obvious reasons pups thus affected should not be bred from as adults.

Guide to Stages of Development

Backline Puppies' front and back ends grow at different rates; between the ages of 3 and 6 months a puppy will usually appear to slope upwards to the hindquarters. If the puppy is proportionately angulated front to rear the front legs will catch-up by about 9 months so that when standing correctly the backline should be level.

Chest Broadens and deepens with age, depending upon maturity rate and environmental factors. A dog's first mating will usually prompt faster maturity.

Coat A puppy's baby coat is usually very thick and fluffy. It begins to change to the adult type coat at around 6 to 7 months of age. The new coat will probably be straighter and flatter as it may lack undercoat until the puppy is about 9 or 10 months old. Undercoat will first appear around the buttocks and on the shoulders. If the adult coat is going to be curly or wavy it will show signs of this by the 6 or 7 months mark.

Borders are known to go 'in' or 'out' of coat at various times of the year, regulated by such factors as the season, 'heat' periods in bitches, diet, trauma. As coats are due to shed they become dry and brittle; some show a tendency to browning on top. It takes approximately 6 to 12 weeks for a bitch to return to good coat after shedding. Dogs tend to exhibit slightly less coat loss.

Chocolate coloured dogs are especially subject to sunbleaching; they will lighten considerably on top.

Blue coloured coats at certain stages can appear slightly straw coloured on the tips.

Blue and red coloured coats tend to darken with maturity, as also does the tan of the tricolour.

Coat length—from about 4 to 7 months puppies appear to be short-coated. However, a Border may take up to 18 months of age (and sometimes longer, depending upon the maturity rate of the line) to grow a moderate length coat with accompanying breeching, feathers and mane.

Ears Ear development is variable and unpredictable. Ear carriage is affected by the puppy's teething process and may change daily from straight up (pricked) to hanging down over the eyes; the ears may also go independently in different directions. Once teething is complete the ears should settle down to their intended carriage, which is not always the position the ears were in when the dog was a puppy (most puppies under 6 weeks have bent-over ears). These may develop to be semi-erect, pricked or heavy. The final look of the ear will depend upon the size, texture and set-on of the ear.

Eyes Puppies are born with blue eyes which gradually darken to brown by about 6 to 8 weeks of age. Occasionally one eye will remain blue but it is usually discernible as different by about 2 weeks of age. Chocolate and blue dogs have considerably lighter brown or amber eyes.

Head development Head proportions are first discernible in puppies under 6 weeks of age, showing as breadth of skull, thickness of muzzle and angle of stop. From 2 to 9 months the head goes through various growth stages and may sometimes appear to go narrow and flat. However, with adulthood the skull broadens out and the stop reappears if it started out that way.

Heat periods Bitches generally have their first full season between 11 and 13 months of age, though in slow maturing lines this may be as late as 15 or 16 months. Occasionally puppies will show minor 'spotting' (bleeding) before 9 months.

Where a number of bitches are kept in close proximity, i.e. in kennels or yards, they tend to 'bring each other in'; probably the smell of the first bitch in season triggers the hormonal response of the others. The most common time between oestrus cycles in Borders is 6 or 7 months, thus they occur approximately twice a year. Border bitches usually have well-regulated heat periods.

Leg length Between 4 and 9 months a Border puppy's legs often appear to be too long for the body and the pup looks gangly. By adulthood it is desirable that the leg-space below the body is slightly more than half the dog's height.

Micturition (a) Stance—all puppies begin with the squatting position for urination but by about the age of 9 months male puppies will begin to adopt the three-legged stance. This usually signifies that the puppy has matured to the stage of being able to mate successfully. (b) Territorial—male dogs will cover the scent of another dog by micturating over it. Their urine carries a chemical which gives off a peculiar odour which the dog uses to mark his territory. Territorial marking begins at about the same time as the puppy starts to lift his leg.

Pigment Rate of pigmentation varies. Some puppies are born with nose pigment while others start with pink noses which slowly change to black, slate or liver. It is not unusual for pink spots on the nose to continue to colour over up to 12 months of age. The presence of pigment should also be checked for around the eyelids, on the pads and on the roof of the mouth.

Teeth Full complement of 42 adult teeth should be present by 7 or 8 months of age, though occasionally the first pre-molars are slower to appear.

Testes May descend and retract throughout puppyhood but should be in place by 6 months of age; in extreme cases they may still come down up to 9 months of age.

Ticking Begins to show up around 3 to 4 months of age as the puppy's first baby fluff drops off. The depth of ticking may vary from a few spots on the front legs or face to all-over flecking in the collar, mane and blaze.

3 Training with a Border Collie

Having decided to become a dog owner, for whatever reason—companionship, protection, showing or trialling—there is one common element; you have a dog in your household and it must be socially acceptable to you, your family and your neighbours. All dogs need a certain amount of basic training; they need to know *their* limits in *your* environment.

When we set out to train our Border Collie, what do we mean? We mean taking a dog with its inbuilt instincts and characteristics and somehow making it fit into our lifestyle. In this section I would like to deal with the basic training needed to equip your Border Collie to live in a household situation while remaining a happy, well adjusted dog.

Border Collies are acknowledged to be one of the most intelligent of all breeds; they learn quickly, they enjoy a challenge and they like to be a useful part of the family. Many people fail to bring a Border Collie to its full potential because of the limits they impose on the dog—and because the owners have not understood that the Border Collie thrives on constant involvement and stimulation.

A Border Collie is intelligent, sensitive, biddable and loyal. Therefore you need to teach your Border Collie its limits under your code of behaviour; the dog will abide by those limits, not because it thinks something is right or wrong but because it senses your pleasure or displeasure; for example, you will never stop a dog from taking unattended food by explaining to him that stealing is wrong! But you can teach the dog not to touch your food all the same. You must teach him that as his pack leader you are in control and *you* won't allow it.

And this is the very essence of dog training.

Limitation training

'Bad habits' (our moral code) are learnt just as easily as desirable ones and like all habits they are very hard to change. Always try to direct your puppy as you would want him as an adult—a little bundle of clean, fluffy puppy looks so cute leaping onto the lounge and lying with his head on his paws or, even cuter, lying with his head over the side! Project this picture one year later and decide if a 22 kg dog with grubby paws and scratchy nails on the lounge is going to be equally appealing! You then have to make the decision and be consistent. If you decide you don't really want the dog on the lounge then don't let him jump on it as a puppy, no matter how cute he looks. As a puppy he can be taught either to jump on the lounge or not to jump on the lounge. The choice is with the pack leader (you).

The age to start training

Most Border Collies learn very quickly. Play training can begin with puppies as young as three or four weeks. By the time the puppy is about six months old he should be coming when called, sitting on command and remaining when left. Play fetching should have already started.

However, I firmly believe that dogs, like children, need their puppyhood to play, explore, develop and generally enjoy life. This enables them to grow into happy, outgoing adult dogs more inclined to enjoy the work that is to come later. I would not begin serious training with a Border Collie under the age of nine months; depending upon the individual dog this may be extended to twelve months or so. I would generally start serious work with a bitch after her first season, but males are usually slower to mature and may not be ready to settle down to serious training until a year or so old. A word of caution though—I feel it is important to have a dog trained in the basics before he is used for stud services; especially if he is to be a trial dog, he should be well and truly aware that his first job in life is working for his master.

Socialisation should have begun by three weeks of age, but as most owners won't acquire their puppy until it is six to eight weeks old, socialisation and play-training in its new home should begin straight away.

Recognising your dog's nature

Before you can successfully train any dog you need to train yourself in the following:
- To know as much as possible about the characteristics of your breed in general.
- To know your own dog and what motivates *him* to learn.
- To recognise your own dog's nature.

The Border Collie is a sheepdog, selectively bred and trained over the years to enhance the following characteristics:
- Herding many types of stock.
- Keeping them in a pack.
- Moving them in a given direction.
- Protecting them.
- Responding to the commands of its owner (pack leader).
- Using his eyes to hold, mesmerise and control stock.

A dog's nature is generally recognised as being 'hard' or 'soft'. By this is meant that some breeds, e.g. the cattle dog, require a very firm hand and strong will to train them to do something that they don't particularly want to do. Hard dogs do not 'go to pieces' with severe discipline and tend to forgive and forget very quickly.

The Border Collie is known by and large as a 'soft' dog—he wants to please his owner and is very sensitive to correction. He knows by the sound of your voice or the look on your face when he has done something wrong. Hard handling (anger and physical reprimands) will cause the Border 'to go to pieces' and he very rarely

forgets! You will recognise a Border 'going to pieces' when his tail goes between his legs, he looks at you in a reproachful way and ends up rolling over into the submitting position. If your correction is having this effect on your dog, then it is too hard. (The exceptional situation would be in the case of an aggressive biter, where hard discipline is called for.) As a general rule I would say that Border Collies should never be hit for correction. Of course, there are degrees of hardness and softness within the breed and each trainer must learn to recognise what works best for a particular dog.

A further division in the character of a Border can be recognised in the 'worker' and the 'innovator'. The worker adopts a very sensible approach to training. Once having understood what you require of him, he simply goes on doing it in a very reliable no-nonsense way. The innovator learns very quickly, often anticipating what is required and doing it before being commanded. He is usually a spectacular trial dog but unreliable because of anticipating or wanting to do something different.

Another special characteristic of the Border is the predisposition to crouch and 'give eye', found more strongly in some lines than others. Thus, if you observe a Border approaching a cat, fowls in the yard or ducks on a dam (or even birds or flies or ants in the backyard), you may see him crouch to the slow-walk position and attempt to mesmerise the substitute flock by keeping his eyes on them as he creeps forward; in a sense commanding them to stay still, maybe using willpower, but certainly projecting it using his eyes. It is as well to note that if a dog has a strong eye he will be concentrating so hard that he may appear to his owner to have gone deaf or to have forgotten all of his training or simply to be very disobedient. In fact, none of these things has happened. Your dog's instincts have simply taken over and the simplest way to break his concentration is physically.

Though having a good eye is definitely an asset in stock work, a Border which is too strong in eye is limited in his usefulness if he cannot be verbally controlled. For the pet or obedience owner this should not be a problem.

How a dog learns

The ability to train dogs is simply the result of understanding the process by which a dog learns and the peculiarities of the individual dog that you are dealing

with. The process is common to all dogs but the way it should be put into effect needs to be adapted for different dogs.

Before beginning training, take special note of the following:

1. The dog is an animal; his capacity for thinking has never been proven, so his trainer must do the thinking for him. However, his instincts for survival, i.e. ensuring a food supply and procreation, can often be harnessed for effective training.

2. The dog is not a moral being; he never does things because he knows they are right or wrong or because he wants to annoy his owner—we impose our moral code on the dog.

3. The dog is a pack animal; when he is transferred from his natural pack to his owner's household the members of that household become his new pack. Instinct and generations of conditioning result in the dog seeking out a pack leader or attempting to become the pack leader! To effectively train a dog the trainer must always remain the pack leader.

The training process

Repetition and praise

This requires the handler to show the dog what you want him to do and then to praise him each time you get him to do the exercise. The dog may need to be shown how to do the exercise over and over again.

Consistency

The handler must be careful to teach the exercise in exactly the same way each time, using the same verbal commands and the same tone of voice. The dog does not really understand the words being used but is associating a sound with an action. Therefore the sound and the action must always be the same to get the same response.

The trained Border Collie keeps fit and enjoys life

Anticipation and correction

Correction is simply training the dog *not* to do something by making it unpleasant for him. If possible the trainer should be watching the dog very carefully and reading the signs—where you can see that a dog is about to do something undesirable, then correct him before he learns that he can break your commands.

Voice variation

A Border Collie is extremely responsive to changes in the tone of your voice; it is sound variations rather than words which the dog understands. The sound of your voice can indicate pleasure, disapproval, firmness, hesitation. A Border Collie can definitely sense when someone is unsure of themselves. This usually ends up with the dog 'trying you out' and doing whatever he chooses as he senses that he may be able to assert himself

as pack leader over you. It is not necessary to shout unless your dog is some distance away. In fact, a keen dog will tune-in to the slightest whisper.

The time and the temper

Border Collies are very sensitive dogs, well tuned in to the feelings of their owners. The most effective training is achieved when your mind is totally on the dog, even if only for a very short period of time. If you are in a hurry, or worried or off-colour you are more likely to run short of patience and act in an inappropriate way, e.g. forget the correct commands, change your voice tone (it is very difficult to be happy and enthusiastic if you are feeling ill!) or lose your temper. Any one of these will serve to confuse the dog and training will not be positive. Indeed to lose your temper with a Border Collie will most likely set back your training several weeks. The Border will remember for a long time the point at which you became very angry and will hesitate at that point in subsequent training. When this happens it is often necessary to start teaching the exercise all over again, making sure to re-establish the dog's confidence in some way, using much encouragement. Furthermore, if your mind is on other things your reaction time slows down. This usually means your corrections are too late or too slow and the dog's training is again set back.

Even a minimum period of five minutes of undivided attention when training will achieve more than a half-hour of inappropriate training.

Staying in control

In many subtle ways Border Collies often train their owners; this often starts out as the trainer's fault but in a sense it ends up as re-establishing who is the pack leader. Some of the signs of this happening might be barking, breaking stays or running away, all of which bring you instantly running back. It is important that you always remain in control—if the dog runs away, you run in the opposite direction and encourage the dog to come to you. Your dog will respect you and work for you as long as you are his pack leader.

Forms of encouragement and correction

If the Border Collie can sense your pleasure then he is satisfied. Praise can take the form of a special phrase such as 'good dog', a pat or a hug, allowing the dog to stand up with his paws on you or to leap into your arms, or a food reward. Again you need to determine what gives your dog the greatest satisfaction. Some dogs are not interested in food rewards at all and prefer a pat, while others will do anything for half a Goodo! Very sensitive dogs may need a lot of exaggerated and enthusiastic verbal and physical encouragement to build up their confidence to accept they are doing the right thing, while the innovator may require the minimum of very gentle praise to keep him calmed down. Whatever your particular dog requires, the important thing is to remember to give the dog some form of encouragement, especially in the early stages of teaching a new exercise. The end of each training session should signal some special time of play or fun—a long walk, a game of ball or whatever.

The only correction a Border Collie usually requires is a firm 'No', or 'Uh-Uh', or whatever word you choose to use which will tell the dog not to do what it was about to do. It is not necessary to shout, especially if the dog is right next to you, but it is important to get a tone of disapproval in your voice.

The most important point to remember about correction is that it must be done *while* the dog is committing the misdemeanour or preferably *before* it actually does the wrong thing. It is impossible to explain to a dog that you are angry with it for something it did five minutes ago. Thus it is important when training a dog to set up a situation where you can give the dog your full attention, which with a Border should be for short periods of time.

Generalisations on training a Border Collie

Timing
A Border Collie learns very quickly, therefore training sessions should be kept short (5–10 minutes) and varied. A Border becomes bored and sour by being asked to do the same thing over and over again.

Fetching
Border Collies are not natural retrievers; fetching is best taught when the puppy is very small and still interested in chasing and pouncing. When the puppy is 3–4 months old, play games such as rolling a ball down a hallway, or squeezing a squeaky toy behind your back and encouraging the puppy to find it.

Heeling
It is natural for a Border Collie to want to walk either wide or forging ahead of its owner. After all, the Border has been bred for generations to work away from its owner, often out of sight. When starting heeling training, chat to your dog to keep it close to you and watching you, giving it an occasional pat on the head or under the chin. When making turns talk the dog around as you go. Use the check chain as little as possible. It may help to carry a favourite toy in your hand and to turn heeling into a game occasionally.

Jumping
In his life as a working dog, a Border will scramble over obstacles rather than jump them—logs, fences, stiles, etc. Borders can jump, and usually enjoy it, but take care when you start jumping training to teach the dog to actually jump rather than scramble. This requires starting with the jumps very low until the dog learns that the command 'Over' means to jump clear.

Training you

It is important, if you tell your Border to do something, that you are in a position to make the dog complete the exercise; if you do not then your Border will quickly learn how to train you.

Anticipation

The Border is well known for the characteristic of anticipation—that is, knowing what you are going to want him to do, and doing it before commanded. This is probably a fine characteristic in all situations except the trial ring, where you need to be always one step ahead! Vary every exercise as much as possible so that you keep the dog guessing. Never work to a set pattern. Try to catch the dog out by doing something unexpected. Not only will this help to break the habit of anticipating but it will also help to maintain interest and enthusiasm.

The recall

A peculiarity of Border Collies is that they do not run in a straight line. When trotting ahead of you, either free or on a long loose lead, a Border will continuously criss-cross your pathway; if free he will run ahead, backtrack and circle you—checking and herding all the time. When called in for a recall most Borders will veer from side to side of an imaginary straight line to their handler. Provided the dog is coming in with enthusiasm, I would not make any attempt to correct this as it should not cost you points in a trial. Attempts to bring the dog in straight usually result in 'creeping'—an extremely slow recall because the dog has become unsure of what is required.

The only point at which correction can be made is to make sure the dog sits straight in front of you. A dog coming in on an angle will tend to sit askew—one way to correct this is to place an obstacle such as parallel planks or your extended leg in front of you so that the dog must come in straight to sit in front of you.

Avoid rough treatment

By and large the Border Collie is a 'soft' dog—very responsive to training but easily cowed by an over-heavy hand or harsh training. If treated too roughly your Border will work reluctantly and lack enthusiasm, but if treated sensibly and intelligently will do anything you ask. These dogs learn quickly and rarely forget.

The check chain

There are differing opinions regarding the use of a check chain in training. My own opinion is that the check chain can be a useful aid provided it is used correctly and carefully. As far as Borders are concerned overuse of the check is definitely not recommended; a Border can be talked into or encouraged to work very easily by the use of praise and pleasurable experience, as the Border is a willing worker and is generally happier doing something. The check chain should be used strictly as a sudden, unexpected correction when the dog is doing something wrong. It is preferable that the dog does not associate the correction with the owner, so that when the dog is brought to the correct position make sure he experiences much praise. The Border shies off harsh correction and my experience in training them is that harsh correction is very, very rarely required.

A word of caution—never leave a check chain on an unattended dog, as dogs have been known to choke or hang themselves when a check chain has caught on fences, pegs, etc. If a dog is to be restrained unattended it is best done using a leather collar.

Play training

As the name suggests, play training involves making use of a puppy's natural instincts and behaviour, from three to four weeks of age onwards, and associating these behaviours with words or signals which your dog will instinctively respond to as an adult. The most important aspect of this is that it must be done as part of the puppy's natural play periods and must remain *fun*, never forced. Young puppies will initiate pounce games with your feet, chasing games, tug-of-war, play fighting, etc. They will usually pick up and run off with something thrown or dropped, or sit up to look at you, and so on. Most of these actions are, in the pup's mind, associated with survival—stalking, pouncing on and running away with imaginary food as they would do in the wild. In this book I have attempted to show you some ways to channel these instincts to achieve a manageable adult. (For more details on the method of puppy play training see Joan Bray and Lisa Brack, *Good Dog: A Guide for the Beginner*, Kangaroo Press, Sydney, 1991)

All early training should be done in a confined area—a fenced backyard or run or perhaps in the kitchen. It is best if there are as few distractions as possible—no wandering cats or playing children. After all a puppy is only a baby; his attention is easily distracted. I find that the hardest problem to overcome is the enthusiasm of the owner, which often leads to overdoing training. Remember, gentle directed learning is all that should be aimed for; always take a lot of pleasure in puppy's achievements but don't try to force him to perform over and over.

Basic training

Come when called

At each mealtime walk a few paces away from puppy with his dinner bowl in your hand, repeatedly saying his name and 'Come' with enthusiasm. As you put his dinner bowl down give him a pat and tell him 'good dog'. Continue to do this at each feeding. Remember, always walk away from the puppy, never towards him. Also, don't try to stand still and call him, even if he is some distance from you, as this is inviting a game—he may run off to see if you will chase him. He is just as happy to chase you. At a later age this element of chase is one of the best ways to bring your dog to you with enthusiasm. Whenever your puppy comes to you, bend down and give him a good pat and an enthusiastic 'good dog' (or whatever words you choose). If puppy happens to be eyeing the cat, digging a hole or in some way is distracted when you come out with his dinner bowl, simply go over to him and attract his attention by touching him under the chin and directing his head towards you—then walk a few paces away, again calling and encouraging. You may even have to pick him up and set him down elsewhere to get his mind off the distraction.

Never for any reason reprimand the puppy, either verbally or physically, when he comes to you. Sometimes this will require a lot of patience. For example, suppose you walk into the backyard and Spot has just finished chewing the end off your towel—your first response is to shout his name. Spot thinks, 'Here is my beloved mistress,' and rushes to you. If you bend down and clout him on the bottom, perhaps screaming at him, 'You bad, naughty dog,' what does Spot learn from this? He learns that he is a bad, naughty dog to run to you when you call his name! He will not associate the reprimand with the misdeed, but only with the calling of his name.

No matter how hard it is, if you call your puppy and he comes the response should always be pleasure and praise. Even if you don't actually call him and he runs up to you, always pat and praise.

Except in unusual circumstances you should never chase your puppy (the chances are that she will outrun or out-manoeuvre you anyway). You will probably end up feeling annoyed and frustrated while the dog has learnt that it can outsmart you and doesn't always have to come when you call.

If for some reason the puppy runs away from you ignore her; if possible, go on doing something else. Her natural curiosity will send her looking for you eventually. Always try to think ahead to avoid the possibility of a problem—e.g. until thoroughly responsive to a call, puppy should only be loose in the safety of an enclosed backyard. If you let puppy loose in a park, for instance, when her great pleasure is in running free, her unbounded curiosity will have her running and leaping all over the place. It is very unlikely that you will teach a puppy to come to you under those circumstances. If you try calling her and she simply runs away then you have allowed her to learn an undesirable response, i.e. that she need only come when she feels like it! Think ahead to avoid negative training situations.

Sit

Again, this may be achieved with a very small puppy using food or the puppy's meal. If you allow the puppy to smell the food and then hold it slightly above and to the back of his head, the normal reaction is for the puppy to sit down and reach his head up towards the food. Immediately give the command 'Sit', give the food and plenty of praise and patting. If the puppy does not sit when you hold the food above his head, an alternative method is to back the puppy into a corner or up against a wall, then gently reach down and sit the puppy with your hands (one hand on the chest, the other behind the back legs) simultaneously giving the command 'Sit'. Again reward with food and praise. If this is done consistently at each feeding, within a very short time the puppy should be sitting when told.

Walking on the lead

For a very small puppy, heeling is really only teaching him to walk on a lead. It is important that a pup become accustomed to being on a lead and that he be socialised by being taken for outings and walks.

It is best not to use a check chain on a young puppy; instead use a leather or webbing collar suited to your dog's size.

1. Put the collar on your puppy and leave it on for several days to allow the pup to adjust to the feel of it around his neck. Don't attempt any lead training at this stage but give the puppy lots of attention, reassurance and game playing while the collar is on.

2. After three or four days, attach a short piece of lightweight cord or webbing; 15 to 45 cm of venetian blind cord will do depending on the size of your pup. Allow him to trail this around for a few minutes at a time when you are watching him. Every now and then, gently hold the lead and encourage the puppy to run along. Do this for only a few seconds and give him lots of excited praise. Remove the 'lead' and release the puppy.

The whole procedure should be done in an enclosed area and should only last three or four minutes. It is important to note that the trailing lead should never be left on the puppy when he is unsupervised as it could get caught on something and cause him injury or discomfort.

3. After several days of 'play training', and when it seems that the puppy is not bothered by the collar or lead, it may be time to start teaching him to walk 'on the lead'. There are several ways to do this, depending on whether your puppy is outgoing and adventurous, or shy and retiring.

The following suggestions for introducing the walk on lead may help avoid problems:

• Carry your pup a short distance away from your yard, e.g. to the end of the block or street, attach the lead and head toward home. The chances are that he will happily race back to familiar territory.

• Carry some appealing food, e.g. cheese or cooked liver, and offer it to the pup as you walk along, intermittently holding it in front of his nose and encouraging him to walk a few paces before giving it to him as a reward. Food is quite useful for shy puppies as it takes their minds off a seemingly threatening situation.

• Introduce lead training away from home, perhaps on a beach (if it allows dogs) or in a park. Transport the pup to a safe area, clip on the lead before taking him out of the car, then carry him to your chosen place and put him on the ground. Use a long, loose lead to do this, so that as he becomes interested in new sights and smells he may happily run off to investigate and will gradually become used to the restriction of the lead.

Lie down

As the dog becomes an adult there may be occasions when you want him to be unobtrusive and quiet, perhaps at meal times. The best way to achieve this is to teach the command 'Lie down' to the young puppy. This is best taught to the puppy when on his own, and perhaps after he has been fed or playing, i.e. at a time when puppy may be tired and ready to rest. I find it useful to have a special mat or blanket and to gently encourage the puppy to lie on it. You may have to hold him in position to begin with and gently stroke his head or chest to soothe and calm him, quietly repeating the command 'Lie down'. This may start off for only a few seconds at a time as it must be understood that the puppy's instincts are to remain on his feet and alert in case of attack. The dog is more vulnerable in the 'down' position and therefore this exercise needs lots of reassurance. When it becomes obvious that the puppy is going to get up, quickly give him a command to release him from lying down, e.g. 'Off you go'. To teach a puppy to lie down will probably take longer than most other exercises. Therefore it should not be rushed or hurried but done with patience and in quiet and familiar surroundings.

Wait

Once a puppy has learnt to sit, he can be taught to 'Wait' simply by telling him to wait and correcting him if he starts to get up. You may wish to teach 'Wait' before you feed him or before letting him out of his pen, doors or the car, or to wait before being allowed outside. This exercise can also be adapted to teach a puppy to remain in a particular area, for example, when indoors. Again, this exercise should proceed slowly, beginning with only a couple of seconds wait and gradually building up in time. It is important to give a release word at the end of the wait period, e.g. 'Off you go'.

Sound a warning

If you watch your puppy very carefully you will see him give some indication when a car pulls up outside or someone is at the gate or door. Usually the ears will lift, the head will move in the direction of the sound and the puppy may actually run towards the door and bark. This can be harnessed with appropriate words, for example, 'Is there someone coming?' in a very excited tone of voice. If the puppy barks or runs to the door give exaggerated praise.

Speak

Again by observing your puppy very carefully you will pick up something which gets your puppy excited or makes him bark. (By and large Border Collies are very quiet dogs and bark very little.) However, it may be that sighting a cat or a bird in a cage, or the sound of a lawn mower will cause the pup to bark. Once the puppy starts to bark, you then try to increase his barking by becoming very excited and giving an appropriate command and praise, e.g. 'Speak, speak'. Always remember to tell the puppy when to stop, e.g. 'That's enough', while closing your hand lightly round his muzzle.

Shake

There are two occasions when a puppy will vigorously shake himself—after being wet or after a sleep. When you see your pup shaking himself, quickly repeat 'shake! shake!' in a high pitched voice. During and after puppy's bath would be a good time to reinforce the shake command. Be prepared to keep this up for many weeks (or months) until your puppy makes the association.

Obviously this list of suggestions is only a guide.

A Border Collie learns very quickly and thrives on stimulation and doing things. I have known Borders trained to 'mind' a baby in a pram, find car keys, carry a purse to the car, bring an egg each day from the fowlyard to the house, put pegs in the peg basket, open gates, doors and slide bolts and many, many more routine activities. The list of exercises you can teach your dog depends upon your own imagination and ingenuity, but I would stress the use of patience and consistency.

A Border Collie is a very sensitive dog, willing to please, but he is still a dog! If he appears not to understand what you want, then the responsibility is on you to find a different method of getting through to him. If you become frustrated, annoyed or angry, give the training session away—trying to train your dog at this time may do more harm than good. Discussing your problem with other dog trainers will usually relieve your frustration and result in a sharing of ideas and finding a solution to your particular problem.

Keep dog training in perspective! It should always be enjoyable for both dog and owner.

Common problems

Through my involvement both as a breeder and as an obedience training instructor, I have often been confronted with so-called 'problem dogs'. The most common problems include:
• Barking unnecessarily
• Digging
• Pulling clothes from the clothes line
• Jumping up on people
• Wearing a track in the lawn
• Not eating
• Chasing cats

No doubt different things can be added to this list but I feel it is fair to say that most problems can be traced to two basic causes—poor training as a puppy and boredom (looking for something to do or trying to get the owner's attention).

A Border Collie is not a lap dog, nor is he a house dog. He is an active, intelligent dog bred to work. This does not mean that he is unsuitable as a household companion—on the contrary, Border Collies make excellent family dogs provided they are part of the family, are well exercised, have things to do and a sense of responsibility. Early training is essential to set the dog its limits. Thus, a young puppy can be easily taught to sit in front when called and reprimanded if he tries to jump up. On the other hand, if a puppy has been encouraged to jump up and be patted when he is small, he does not understand that you don't want his big, dirty feet on your clean clothes when he is older!

Such things as tracking the yard, pulling clothes off the line and barking are sure signs of boredom. The dog is simply looking for something to do! Usually the track is the result of herding birds or cars, i.e. following his instincts. Flapping clothes on a line simply invite a game.

There is no simple solution to any of these problems, particularly if they have developed over a long period of time and have become a habit. Each dog and each problem needs to be considered individually, but the following points may help you avoid future problems:
• Teach a puppy its limits.
• Exercise the dog and give him plenty of things to do with his owner or family; give your Border a sense of responsibility and interest in life.
• Take steps to prevent the problem occurring, e.g. if you know you are going to be away for the day and you have washing on the line, confine the dog away from the clothes line.

To correct problems which have already become established often requires ingenuity and always requires your constant attention. Correction must be given absolutely at the point at which the dog is committing the undesirable act. For example, a correction for pulling clothes from the line must occur the very instant the dog starts to jump up at the clothesline! To attempt to correct him even five minutes later is too late—the dog will not understand your words about 'tearing the clothes off the line'. All he knows is that you are angry with him for whatever he is doing at that time, which may be simply sleeping in the sun. The dog becomes confused and instead of greeting you when you return home he may stay out of your way expecting a reprimand!

It can sometimes be useful to set up a problem situation in order to correct it.

Many problems occur as a result of the owner's absence. A dog may become a habitual barker when the owner is out. To correct this type of problem often requires the assistance of friends to act in your absence. It is important here to examine your lifestyle in relation to owning a dog. A dog left often on his own and confined will become bored and frustrated, and may bark simply for something to do! Sometimes a second dog for a playmate may be the answer.

Whatever the problem, there is certainly no set list of solutions. The solution will only be found when recognising the cause of the problem. Thus, if the problem is boredom then no amount of smacking or shouting will solve the problem; it may stop one manifestation of the problem such as digging but the chances are the dog will find something else to do. It should be re-emphasised here that the dog does not have a code of ethics—it is not being naughty just to annoy you! The dog's actions are the result of either instinct or training. In my experience there are very few 'problem' Border Collies—most often the problem is an unthinking owner.

Dog Obedience Trialling

Dog Obedience Trialling is an active outdoor sport which is enjoyed by people of all ages. Basically, the dog is taught a series of exercises and when competent is tested by an Obedience Judge at a recognised trial.

One way to make a start in this sport is to join an Obedience Club. A list of these can be obtained through the Kennel Control in your state. Border Collies have proven themselves worldwide as popular and top obedience dogs. They learn quickly and enjoy this 'work'.

For a more complete guide to basic and obedience training see *'Good Dog': A Guide for the Beginner*, by Joan Bray and Lisa Brack, Kangaroo Press, 1991.

4 Show Fever

There are a number of routes to the show ring for a Border Collie. Breeders plan litters for many reasons: to replace ageing stock, and maintain a blood line; with the aim of producing a big show winner; to fulfil an order from another breeder (also hopeful of acquiring a major show winner, or a particular blood line); to have their stock presented in the show ring and so build up their kennel name.

The majority of show people start out simply as dog-lovers who, having answered a 'Border Collie For Sale' ad in the newspaper come away convinced that they have a potential show champion on their hands. The breeder may believe that a pup so purchased has potential. In the hope of seeing the outcome the breeder may either suggest it be shown or, if the buyer is reluctant to become involved, may retain the papers and offer to show the pup himself. It is probably as well to point out that if the breeder believes that the pup is a 'one in a million' he is not very likely to sell it!

Can a beginner buy an oustanding show pup? There are many factors to be considered here, not the least being the state of the market, the breeder's stock capacity and the degree of buyer's luck! Most well-bred litters will contain more than one potential show champion. Certainly a breeder will endeavour to find show homes for his best puppies. If the market is oversupplied then it is very likely that show quality pups will be sold as pets and never see the show ring. Others may be sold on the condition that they be shown.

Some breeders like to 'run-on' puppies to assess their show potential at a later date. Some have the capacity (yarding, feeding, council regulations, etc.) to be able to do this, perhaps selling off stock somewhere between six and twelve months of age. Another approach is to sell older dogs, perhaps aged six years and up, to make way for young show stock. Many breeders feel that they cannot part with family pets in this way, but still wish to continue to breed and so will sell show quality pups.

It is as well to remember that while most litters contain a number of pups 'able to be shown' (indeed, barring major faults, to be discussed later, all pups can be shown), not all pups, even good quality pups, will become champions, and even less will have the outstanding qualities required for show 'greatness'. My observation has been that breeders will produce many litters over many years to achieve that one outstanding 'In Show' winner. Breeders with the experience to assess their puppies very rarely sell one which shows this kind of potential.

What makes a good show dog?

There are three main considerations here—compliance with the breed standard, ring presence and the handler.

Breed standard

The Australian National Kennel Council (ANKC), the governing body for pure bred dogs in Australia, has set down breed standards for the various breeds.

The first responsibility of the breed judge is to ensure that his/her selection of winners exhibit the characteristics laid down in the breed standards, that is, that they conform to type.

Sometimes this is confused with the idea of a particular type in a show line-up. You may hear the remark, 'That judge does not like my type', or 'I can see what she is choosing as type'. To give a very simple but valid

Puppies at four weeks of age:

Above: Black
Top right: A chocolate and a blue in the foreground with a lilac in the background
Right: Pair of lilac puppies—the colour starts out a pale silver grey and darkens

Six week old puppies from the same litter showing a range of colours—black, chocolate, lilac and a blue tricolour

Colour range from puppy to adult:

Above: Blue at six weeks
Above right: at six months, and
Right: as a young adult

Left: Lilac at six weeks, and *Above:* the same puppy at eight months, still showing her juvenile coat. Note that the eye and nose colour tones with the coat

Top left: Red puppies at six weeks
Above: A different red puppy at six months showing more depth of colour

Left: Red tends to darken with maturity. This is the puppy on the left in the photo above, at the age of twelve years. Note the black nose and dark brown eyes

Red can range in tone from wheaten to the deep ginger of this bitch

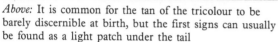

Above: It is common for the tan of the tricolour to be barely discernible at birth, but the first signs can usually be found as a light patch under the tail

Above right: Tricolour (black, white and tan) well marked at six weeks

Right: Tricolour youngster in the 'gangly' stage

Below and below right: Distinctive tan markings on black tricolour may also be found in chocolate and blue tricolours

example, among Border Collies one sees at least two distinct groupings (for want of a better word)—dogs which are slightly shorter in leg, stocky in body and have very profuse coats and others which have slightly longer legs, longer bodies and much less coat. Both groups conform to the standard with regard to height, length of body and coat description.

So which is correct? This depends upon the judge's interpretation of 'exhibiting the characteristics of the breed standard'.

Of course, what we are looking at here is a surface picture; it must be remembered that the whole of the standard must be considered when deciding whether or not a dog conforms to type. As the breed standard is the most important document when considering the show Border Collie, it is dealt with fully in Chapter 5. Thus, the 'good' show dog is the one which comes the closest to embodying the requirements of the standard.

On the other hand, though the standard does specify some undesirable faults it does not evaluate them, and so an outstanding dog with an obvious fault may still win over a mediocre dog without that particular fault. In other words, faults are not outright disqualifying factors (except in the case of a lack of entirety).

The most common procedure is to assess each animal as a whole and compare it with its competitors on the day. Individual preferences and, I suspect, fashions or fads, play some part in determining winning stock.

The novice at showing is advised to study the standard carefully, recognise that there is much left unstated and to develop an eye for a good dog.

Ring presence and presentation

Without a doubt some dogs compel you to look at them. Presentation, of course, is important. Exhibitors can give themselves a better chance with good grooming and pre-ring preparation and training (see next section). A dog would have to be outstanding indeed to win in a dirty, unkempt condition.

However, 'presence' is something else again. It manifests itself in different ways. Some dogs sparkle and are alert, your eyes continually return to them, they compel your interest. They may be very happy, active dogs, though completely under the control of the handler. Presence can also show itself as a very gracious, almost regal, bearing—a dog standing with its head held high, its feet firm and its back straight, coat gleaming—its whole demeanour saying, 'Look at me, I'm special'.

The handler

A good show type should conform to the standard, it helps if the dog has ring presence, but without doubt the handler has some influence on the final outcome. A poor handler can disadvantage a good dog while a good handler can make a good dog stand out. Of course it is desirable that the best specimen, the most 'typey' dog, should win. But what has to be remembered is that in a show line up there are often several equally good dogs, each with their own good points, each with their own faults. In these instances, the way the dog is handled can make the difference between first and second. Good handling is the result of experience and practice and is further discussed in the next section.

If you like dogs, you enjoy being outdoors and you are reasonably active (and some people would say quite mad!), then showing Border Collies as a sport or a hobby can be and should be lots of fun. So far dog showing still ranks as an amateur pursuit, and as such allows many people of all ages to have a lot of fun throughout the year. I feel, though, that there are three essential elements to enjoying this hobby. First and foremost, never lose sight of the fact that you are dealing with living, feeling, sensitive animals, who have no interest in (or indeed no concept of) winning or losing at dog shows but simply want to be your companions. Being a Border Collie your companion will go on doing just what you ask of it, until the day it dies if need be. Secondly, one must learn to win with humility and to lose graciously. Lastly, do your best for yourself and your dog but keep in mind that dog showing is a hobby, a leisure time activity—and have fun.

Preparation for the show ring

Both good and average dogs benefit from being presented correctly in the ring. As I see it there are six ongoing steps involved for those few minutes in the ring—good health, grooming, cleanliness, training, show day procedure and ring etiquette.

Health

Of all the breeds the Border Collie, like his blood-brothers the Australian Cattle Dog and the Australian Kelpie, is first and foremost a working dog. The standard

This dog is nearly correct, but is slightly forward on the front feet. Note good length of neck; the back legs are parallel and well spaced

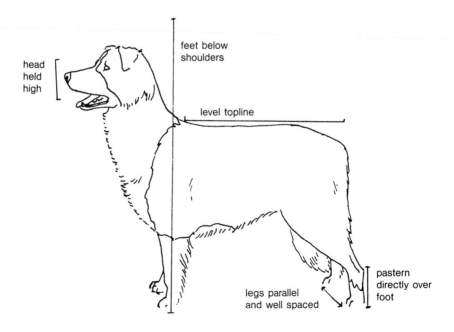

Correct stance

Incorrect stance: Hind legs stretched too far back, head too low, ears flat

Incorrect stance: Hind legs not back far enough and unevenly placed, topline not stretched out level, front legs too far apart, head not held high

Left: Inappropriate feeding led to this bitch being underweight. Note the tucked-up appearance.
Right: Several weeks on a changed diet results in the body filling out and the bitch showing more graceful lines

requires that the Border Collie be of 'sufficient substance to ensure that it is capable of enduring long periods of active duty in its intended task as a working sheep dog'.

No amount of bathing or grooming will cover up for a dog which is in poor health or poor condition. Some of the questions that I am most commonly asked concern feeding. What should I feed my dog? How much should he eat? What can I give him to make his coat grow? How can I get condition on my dog, he won't eat?

Diet has probably been slightly over-exaggerated as affecting the dog's external appearance. Of course it is true that a well fed, healthy dog will have a shining coat, clear, sparkling eyes, a good feel to the body, strong sound teeth, pleasant breath and firm stools and an abundance of energy. Dogs which are poorly fed, overweight or underweight often appear listless, dull in coat (which no amount of sprays can cover), heavy-eyed and generally lack sparkle. The Border Collie standard does not specify weights but it is generally accepted that 15–20 kg (30–45 lb) is average for bitches and 18–24 kg (45–60 lb) for dogs, keeping in mind age, frame and height.

Puppies will often carry a little more weight than necessary; this is rapidly used up during growth periods, when the puppy will become very long-legged and thin-bodied, a stage known as the 'ganglies' (page 54). Thickness of bone will have a bearing on the dog's weight; a light-boned 48 cm male would probably be quite overweight at 24 kg while his heavier-boned brother at 53 cm could probably carry that weight quite well. How then can you assess your own dog's food requirements and condition?

Firstly you must learn to feel beyond the dog's coat. Some Border Collies have quite profuse coats and still have a very firm lean body underneath. Run your hands firmly along the dog's side from chest to butt. If the ribs and backbone protrude and the flank tucks in then the dog is probably too lean for showing. If the muscles are well developed and hard, and the dog has limitless reserves of energy, then it is probably in top working condition. On the other hand, if you cannot feel the ribs but can take hold of a good fistfull of tissue, or if the dog's body is the same width across the shoulders, flanks and buttocks, he is probably too heavy. A good time to really look at your dog's condition is when you bathe him.

A healthy dog in the peak of condition should feel firm and muscular (not fat or ribby) and should curve in gracefully at the flank.

There are many good feeding guides available and much expert help. Talking to a number of show people will reveal varied approaches to diet: dry dog food, canned dog food, fresh meat—cooked or raw, vegetarian or herbal diets, table scraps or human foods.

Most reputable breeders provide their own 'tried and true' feeding chart with puppies that they sell and they usually have recommendations for adult dogs as well.

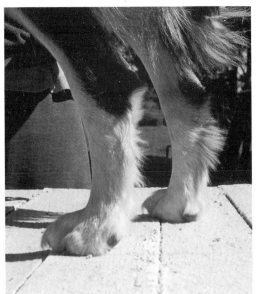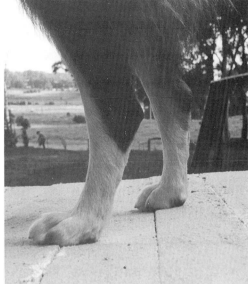

Hind legs and feet untrimmed (left) and trimmed (right)

Experience will indicate the diet that will keep your dog in good health and condition. Perhaps the most widely accepted diet among Border Collie breeders is a 2 to 1 mix of complete dry dog food and fresh meat, with various additives.

Point to keep in mind are:
• Adult dogs require only one feed per day.
• Table scraps shoult not be given to the dog throughout the day but collected and counted as part of the dog's daily rations.
• Avoid titbits—they are only satisfying your need to pander to your dog and usually lead to an overweight, unhealthy animal.
• Vary your dog's diet. Vary the brands of dry dog food used, the types of meat (lamb, chicken, rabbit, etc.).

The foundations of a healthy, well-boned adult dog, of correct height and proportions, begin with the correct feeding of the puppy as outlined in Chapter 1. The right diet and exercise all year round will help to maintain a dog in good show condition. However, there are times when a show dog's diet may need to be varied to suit a special situation:
• When a bitch is shedding coat or recovering from a litter, additional meat, oils or vitamins are required. Various coat improvers (oil and vitamin mixtures) are available.

• Approximately six weeks before a special show, when the animal is required to be at its peak, the proportions of fresh meat to dry dog food may be varied to 50/50 and additional egg yolk may be included to help improve coat sheen.
• When a dog or bitch is confined and unable to be exercised (perhaps as a result of an injury or being 'in season') the food intake may need to be reduced so that the animal does not gain excess weight.

Along with correct feeding, adequate exercise and a stimulating environment will go a long way to ensuring that a Border Collie is kept in top show condition.

Grooming

A Border Collie is a 'low maintenance' dog and requires very little in the way of grooming. A good, straight coat of the correct texture will rarely mat or tangle. However, every dog will enjoy a once-a-week brushing and combing. Particular attention should be given to the long hair around the ears, neck and breeches and along the underside of the tail where 'dags' tend to form. These areas should be combed regularly and the dead hair removed. It is customary to trim the feet, removing the long hair around the foot and between the pads, so that the foot presents a compact and tidy appearance (see previous page). Also, the hind leg, from the hock down, is usually trimmed smooth at the back (but don't touch the front feathers).

If the dog is exercised on a roadway or concrete path the toenails may wear down naturally, otherwise they may need to be clipped. Special clippers are available for this purpose.

Allowing your dog to eat dry, unsoaked kibble or an occasional large raw bone should ensure the teeth remain clean and healthy. If a build-up of yellow-brown deposit occurs, the teeth may need scraping, best done by a vet or experienced dog person.

Cleanliness

The day before the show the dog should be bathed; use a good shampoo and rinse well. Individual preference and experience with your own dog's coat will determine what type of soap, shampoo, conditioner or rinse to use, but the aim is to show a clean, sparkling dog with a shine to his coat and tidied up to as close to perfection as possible. Bathing the dog the day before the show (provided you can keep him clean overnight) enables the natural oils to return to the dog's coat by the following day so that a good brushing, preferably with a pure bristle brush, should bring the coat to a good sheen. If your dog is losing coat or just starting to recover after a moult, bathing on the day of the show may help the coat to fluff-up and appear a little more dense.

Training

The purpose of a dog show is to judge your dog against the dogs of other competitors. To do this the dog must be able to stand to be examined and to move around the ring on a lead to show off his gait. If you begin showing with a puppy then, as long as the puppy has been socialised and taught to walk on a lead, both puppy and handler will gain in confidence the more shows that are attended. There is an art to standing and moving a dog for show purposes; the breeder from whom you obtained your puppy could perhaps advise you on this. The illustrations on pages 56–57 demonstrate correct and incorrect stance.

When a dog is standing correctly the neck is stretched upwards and slightly back and the head is held high; the front legs are straight and parallel and the feet are directly under the shoulder-line; the body is extended and the backline is straight; the back pasterns are parallel when checked from behind and in line with the sides of the body; neither too close nor too far apart.

As far as movement is concerned the dog must gait smoothly and correctly. This type of movement is explained in Chapter 5, along with the most common faults found in the show ring. To improve on both stance and movement, the novice is advised to carefully watch the experienced handler at shows and then to practise, perhaps with the assistance of a mirror or an obliging friend.

Show day procedure

1. Dress appropriately in comfortable, neat clothing, keeping in mind that you will probably have to bend over your puppy, and flat shoes for running round the ring.
2. Arrive in good time to find your ring; walk your dog around to familiarise him with new sights and smells and if necsesary to 'empty out'. A dog will perform better in the ring if he is not preoccupied with trying to find a spot to relieve himself. If the dog does defaecate remember to clean up the mess. Small shovels (known as 'pooper scoopers') are provided at ringside for this purpose.
3. Bring your numbered card and a pin or clip as your number must be worn while you are in the ring. The ring steward will call this number when it is time for you to go into the ring.
4. As showing can be a long procedure it is wise to provide your puppy with drinking water from home; a change in water may cause an upset tummy. A large umbrella for shade, a fold-up chair and a small peg to secure your dog will make a long day more pleasant.

Ring etiquette

To ensure your time in the ring is a pleasure and not an embarrassment the following unwritten rules are usually observed:
1. Do not initiate conversation with the judge. You may be required to answer simple questions such as how old your dog is, and replies should be kept to a minimum. Under no circumstances should you tell the judge your dog's kennel name or previous performance.
2. Gently restrain enthusiastic puppies from jumping on or licking the judge. Biting by dogs of any age is

definitely not allowed and may result in the offending exhibit being asked to leave the ring.

3. Handle a timid puppy very gently and patiently in the ring, accepting that you may have to lose placings until the puppy becomes ring-trained. Socialisation before puppy begins showing may help to reduce this problem.

4. Clean up any mess your dog may make.

5. Conversation with fellow exhibitors should be undertaken quietly and kept to a minimum, making sure to keep your attention on the judge at all times. Conversation between an exhibitor in the ring and persons outside the ring should not occur.

6. Accept the judge's opinion gracefully and lose with a smile, resolve to learn and improve.

Depending on your class and your result, you may be required in the ring a second time. Explain to the steward if you are a new exhibitor and check what is required of you. By and large, dog show stewards are friendly, helpful people.

How to enter a dog show

(*Note:* The following information on entering a show and the showing process is applicable to New South Wales—rules in other states may differ slightly.)

1. The dog must be registered with the New South Wales Canine Council (NSWCC) and the registered owner must also be a member of that body.

2. As a member you will receive the Kennel Control journal. Each month this journal includes current show schedules.

3. Obtain a book of show entry forms from the NSWCC. A completed form, self-addressed envelope and cheque are then sent to the secretary of the show you wish to enter. The details will be found in the schedule. Your ticket(s) will be sent back to you prior to the day of the show. The classes you may enter are listed on the back of the show entry form. It is usual to enter a dog in one class only, even though he may be eligible for several. The reason for this is that if you win one class but are beaten in the other class your dog is eliminated from the Challenge section.

The show process

One aim of showing a dog is to gain 100 Challenge points and so make the dog a Show Champion. The procedure involved in New South Wales is as follows:

1. The winners from each class, except Baby Puppy class, return to the ring to be judged against each other; the judge selects one of this group to receive the Challenge points.

2. The dog Challenge is judged separately from the bitch Challenge.

3. Currently points are awarded as 6 plus one for each dog actually beaten (absent dogs are not counted).

4. The Challenge dog and Challenge bitch then compete against each other to determine the Best of Breed Border Collie. This dog is required to compete again in the Working Dog Group. If the Border Collie should win the Best in Group, he would then go on to compete in the Best in Show line-up which consists of each of the seven individual group winners. Challenge points change with subsequent wins of this nature.

5. After selection of the Best of Breed Border Collie, the winning dog and winning bitch of each class, including Baby Puppy class, compete against each other to represent that class in the Group judging (but Class wins do not earn Challenge points).

6. Other minor awards are also made.

5 The Standard and the Real Thing

It must be very obvious to anybody showing a Border Collie, from beginners to experienced, that some look quite different from others! As I see it, some fairly distinct groupings occur:
• Dogs/bitches on the upper end of the height scale, substantial in bone, broad in head, heavy or 'rose' ears, medium length straight coat.
• Dogs/bitches on the upper end of the height scale, lighter in bone, finer in head, more length to the muzzle, ears variable, medium length straight coat.
• Dogs/bitches on the lower end of the height scale, substantial in bone, medium to broad heads, moderate to high semi-erect ears, profuse coats both straight and wavy.
• Dogs/bitches on the lower end of the height scale, medium in bone, profuse in coat and square in proportions.

These are very broad, non-exclusive groupings, as some animals will exhibit characteristics from one or more of the group classifications. An understanding of how these separate groups' appearances have developed may make us less critical and more understanding of dogs different to our own and of judges' decisions.

So, is any one person's opinion more correct than others? Not necessarily. Breeders, exhibitors and judges can all read and interpret the standard. It would be advantageous to the breed if judges, breeders and exhibitors could interpret, the standard into the same dog in the same way as each other, as this would eliminate the extremes and unify the breed into a recognisable type.

One of the major differences between the Border Collie and most of the benched breeds lies in the fact that the Border Collie was always first and foremost a working dog; by this I mean that he was brought to Australia and bred and developed by farmers, graziers,

stockmen and pastoralists, not by show exhibitors at all. Obviously his appearance was of far less importance than his ability to do his job well.

Secondly, a breed standard did not come with the dog (as it has for most other breeds originating, for example, in Great Britain, Germany, Hungary, America, etc.). Thus the standard for the Border Collie arose in an 'ad hoc' fashion. Though Border Collies were 'shown' as early as 1907, the first Australian National Kennel Council's (ANKC) standard for the Border Collie was not adopted until 1963. Prior to this, Border Collies were exhibited in the various states under separate standards, drawn up in the main by one or two knowledgeable exponents of the breed but with no attempt at overall consensus.

Thirdly, although the breed was much loved by those who owned Border Collies, but was not fashionable as a show dog in those early days, being considered more of a farm dog by the general public, its development was fairly isolated within each state and not unnaturally related to a number of indigenous factors within each state. In Victoria the dogs developed longer, thicker coats to cope with the cold; in Queensland they were mainly lighter in coat and frame, having to contend with hot weather and covering longer distances when working. It is only within the past fifteen years that we have been seeing an increased movement of dogs between the states, probably due to an increase in popularity of the Border Collie and to a much greater willingness of both exhibitors and judges to travel interstate.

Another important factor has been the numerous changes which have been made over the years to the breed standard(s). I believe that these changes were inevitable as the breed evolved and developed and in view of the lack of a unified attempt to assess the breed in its formative years of development as a bench dog.

However, it must be obvious that very carefully breeding for certain characteristics must of necessity take several generations; many years are lost when changes in standard are made. A simple example regarding ear carriage illustrates this point.

Ear shape and carriage were never of any importance to the farmers who worked the Border Collie; as long as the ears resisted dirt and grass seeds and moved sufficiently to tune in to signals and sounds, their appearance was ignored. A comparison of old photographic records shows ears ranging from heavy to pricked and quite often two different ear types on the one dog. The earliest known standard specified 'Ears: small, not set too closely, semi or rose'; the first standard for New South Wales allowed semi-erect or rose ears, but the first ANKC standard of 1963 specified 'Ears: of medium size, set well apart and carried semi-erect'. With such a background it is not surprising to find very little conformity in the ear carriage of Border Collies, and furthermore quite a deal of disagreement as to what exactly is meant by 'semi-erect', and further disagreement as to what type of ears a Border Collie *should* have— high-set, rose, heavy, semi-erect, button or pricked (regardless of the requirement of the standard). The points of unwritten agreement appear to be that the ears lift and move and are sensitive in their use, and that the ears are a minor consideration in the overall appearance of the head.

Thus, considering the history of the breed in Australia, its isolation between states and the piecemeal development of the Standard it is not unnatural that Borders have developed as distinct types, each with their own following and each following quite sure that their type is right.

The terminology of the Standard

As with any technical document, a Breed Standard uses the language of its discipline, terminology which conveys a specific meaning to its readers. All members of the dog fancy should aim to master the basic terminology.

Angulation   Correctly refers to any angle formed at a joint by the bones. However it is most commonly used with reference to Border Collies to describe:
(a) the angle formed by the shoulderblade and the upper arm (forequarter angulation), and
(b) the angle designated by the stifle joint in the hindquarters, i.e. formed by the femur (thigh bone) and the bones of the lower leg.

If an animal has angulation close to that considered anatomically desirable, it is referred to as 'well-angulated' (forequarters), or 'showing a good turn of stifle' (hindquarters). See pages 75 and 78.

Back/topline   The back is the area designated by the interval between the withers and the loin. The topline extends from the back of the head to the tail set and is viewed as part of the profile of the dog.

Balance   The overall appearance of each part of the dog relative to all other parts. The dog is referred to as 'well balanced' when all parts look right together.

Bite   The position of upper and lower teeth when the mouth is closed. The Border Collie is required to have a 'scissor bite', i.e. the lower teeth behind and just touching the inside surface of the upper teeth.

Blaze   The white stripe running up the middle of the dog's muzzle to between the eyes. An 'extended blaze' is one that continues up over the skull to join with the collar at the back of the dog's head.

Bone   Usually refers to the thickness of the dog's leg bones, especially the front legs. 'Well-boned' is usually a requirement of 'substance'.

Breeching   The long hairs found on the inside of the thighs and the back of the buttocks.

Buttocks   The muscular area bounded by the pelvis, croup and upper thigh.

Chest   The area of the body enclosed by the ribs. Depth of chest refers to the distance between the withers and the lowest point of the sternum (breastbone). A reference point for the depth of chest is the position of the sternum in relation to the elbows.

Coarse   Has two meanings:
(a) a dog which is lacking in refinement, i.e. excess muscle development, too heavy in bone and body proportions, and
(b) a harsh, rough feel to the coat.

Condition   State of health and fitness.

Conformation   The way the dog is put together and how this measures up against the requirements of the standard.

Coupling   The area between the lower end of the chest or rib cage and the start of the hindquarters.

Crabbing   An incorrect form of movement in which the rear portion of the dog's body is not travelling in line with the direction of movement. (See page 82.)

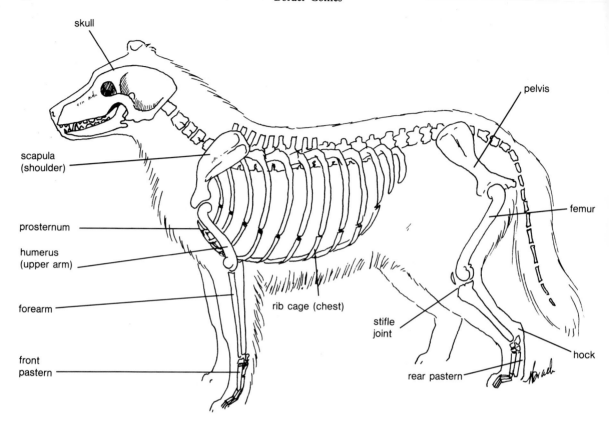

Skeletal system of the Border Collie

Croup   The muscular area above and to the side of the tail-set.

Dentition   Refers to the number of teeth, which in the Border Collie is 42, and their positioning in the jaw.

Dewclaw   The fifth digit or the equivalent of the 'big toe' or thumb, found on the inside of the pasterns.

Elbow   The joint of the front leg between the upper arm and forearm. 'Out-at-elbow' occurs when the front legs, instead of being straight and parallel, have elbow joints turning outwards from the body.

Expression   Refers to how the dog 'comes across', especially looking at the head overall. Expression is what can be read from the dog's eyes, ear set, and movement, head proportions, temperament, 'signals', e.g. lip curling, inquisitiveness, and manifestations of alertness or intelligence. Words used to describe expression in a Border Collie are:

(a) *Alert*—the dog which lifts and moves its ears and is continually looking around and tuning in to signals and sounds. Care must be taken not to confuse stationary semi-erect ears as indicative of alertness.

(b) *Soft*—the face of the dog which gives the impression of a gentle and sweet nature.

Feathering   The longer hair found on the ears, back of the front legs and tail.

Flank   The fleshy area along the side of the dog's body which spans the end of the abdominal region and the hindquarters.

Forearm   The section of the front leg between the elbows and the wrist.

Foreleg   Inaccurately but commonly used to describe the front leg from the elbow to the foot.

Forequarters   The combined front limb, from the top of the shoulder blade (point of withers) to the foot.

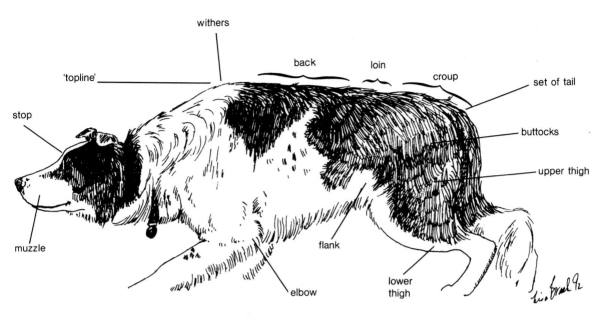

Identifying the parts of the body

Front The assembly of the dog when viewed from head on—forequarters, chest, shoulderline.

Gait Covers the various patterns of movement. (More fully dealt with on pages 80–82.)

Height/height at the shoulder Refers to the vertical measurement of the dog from withers to the ground when the dog is standing correctly.

Hind leg Back leg assembly from pelvis to paw.

Hindquarters Whole of the rear assembly covering the hind legs and thighs.

Hock Corresponds to the ankle joint and heel, thus is found on the hind leg. (*Note:* the word 'hock' is often used incorrectly when referring to the area at the back of the pastern.) To achieve a hock 'well let down' requires a shortened metatarsus bone, i.e. a shortened pastern will bring the 'point of hock' closer to the ground.

Laid-back Refers to the slope of the shoulderblade in relation to the body.

Mane/Ruff The long hair around a Border Collie's neck.

Mismarked Refers to a Border Collie with white markings in undesirable areas, e.g. across the cheeks, around the eyes, on the body.

Muzzle That part of the dog's face composed of the nose and mouth.

Occiput A point on top and to the back of a dog's skull.

Oestrus The same as 'in season' or 'on heat', with reference to the time when a bitch is able to be mated.

Pads Thick mounds of skin on the bottom of the dog's foot.

Pastern Usually used to refer to that length of the front leg between the foot and the first joint.

Pigment Refers to the colour of a dog's skin and is usually used with reference to the nose, lips and pads.

Set-on Refers to the positioning of the tail relative to the buttocks and the positioning of the ears relative to the front of the face.

Soundness In a Border Collie refers to a dog possessing all the necessary physical and mental attributes for it to function correctly as a working dog. Thus, a sound dog is well put-together, fit, healthy, alert and has the instinct to work.

Sternum   The breastbone.

Stifle   The joint in the hindleg which is the equivalent of the knee. 'Turn-of-stifle' is the expression more commonly used and refers to the curve evident in the upper hind leg when the dog is standing.

Stop   The section between the eyes where an angle is formed between the end of the muzzle and the start of the skull (forehead).

Substance   Refers to a desirable size and thickness of bone, body and muscle.

Temperament   The nature and character of the dog, most often used in reference to a dog being approachable, aggressive, nasty or timid.

Topline   See Back.

Tuck-up   The curve of 'belly-line' from the end of the rib-cage to the region of the groin or towards the hindquarters.

Type   Strictly means a dog which conforms to the breed standard. Often used loosely when referring to a group of dogs which are similar to each other and designated a 'type'.

Wall-eye   A lightish blue eye colour.

Withers   Defined by the uppermost point of the shoulder blades.

The Standard

The Standard could be regarded as the master plan towards which breeders, judges and exhibitors should be working. The Standard is the guideline against which each dog presented in the ring is assessed. However, there are several possible variables to be considered when it comes to using the Standard as an assessment for our dogs.

• The Standard is not prescriptive, that is, it does not lay down absolutes in the details of some parts; for example, 'body, moderately long' raises the question: How long is moderately long?

• The Standard assumes a considerable degree of handed-down knowledge among Border Collie owners and a certain amount of 'dog sense'. This can be difficult for the newcomer to acquire.

• Assessing a dog to the Standard must result ultimately in some subjectivity.

What I hope to achieve in this section is to clarify various parts of the Standard, so that readers may have at least a common starting point on which to base their judgments. (It goes without saying that this is *my opinion*.) The way I interpret the *intention* of the standard has been built up as a result of my involvement with Show and Trial dogs since 1970; there has been a vast amount of input from many, many people over the years—all those people who were prepared to answer my questions and share their knowledge with me and to them I owe a great debt. I would not expect full agreement with what I set down here but I write in honesty and good faith; if a sufficient number of people disagree with my assessment of the Standard then I would hope that some fruitful discussions would ensue.

1. General appearance

Key words: Well proportioned, perfect balance, sufficient substance
Faults*: Coarseness, weediness

Comment: The dog should 'look right' overall; stand back and assess the dog as a whole unit—is he all in proportion? e.g. is his head the right size for his body? (*Note:* taken separately the dog could have a smaller than desirable head but still it may balance with the rest of the dog.) Does the length of the dog's legs look right or do they look too short/long for the rest of the body?

All parts of the dog should appear to harmonise with each other, so that no individual part appears out of place.

When determining substance it is usual to consider:
• The lower front leg—does it feel sound, strong and with a degree of depth. If the bone feels thin or fragile or the legs have a skinny appearance then the dog is said to be fine boned. On the other hand, the bone can be too thick, giving the impression of a heavy, cloddy animal, when the description would be 'coarse'.

---

*The use of the word 'fault' is for consistency in reference only. In some sections of the standard faults are specified, while elsewhere they are implied only. What is intended here is to highlight departures from what is desirable. The ANKC standard specifies that any departure from the given points be regarded as a fault; the seriousness of the fault is 'in exact proportion to the degree'.

A well proportioned bitch standing and moving. Movement requires minimum lift of the feet and good reach from the front matched by drive from the hindquarters

• Depth and breadth of chest—obviously, being a working dog, chest capacity is important to a Border Collie. The ability to expand the lungs is essential to enable a continuous, full supply of oxygen to the bloodstream, thus enabling a good dog 'to endure long periods of active duty in its intended task as a working sheep dog'.

The standard describes the chest as 'fairly deep and moderately broad'. As a guide, in a mature adult dog the lowest point of the forechest should come close to the point of the elbow between the front legs. By 'moderately broad' is meant the width of the chest between the shoulders or upper arm, which should be the maximum possible while not interfering with the dog's ability to move, i.e. neither narrow nor too broad.

• Body proportions from withers to buttocks—when viewed from the top, the sides of the body should run almost parallel from shoulder to the pelvic girdle (hips).

Thus, the overall impression of sufficient substance should be given by a strong, sound dog which looks built to cover distances and time.

The specified departures from the desired Border Collie are:

• Coarseness—probably best described as 'too much of everything' so that the impression is not one of a graceful, well balanced active dog but one of a heavy or ungainly appearance.

• Weediness—results from fineness in bone, body and head proportions. Also described among Border Collie people as 'rangy' or 'lacking in substance'.

2. Characteristics

Key words: Highly intelligent, instinct to work, alert expression, loyal, faithful, kindly disposed towards stock. *Faults:* Any aspect of structure or temperament foreign to a working dog.

Comment: This would have to be one of the most important sections in the standard but the one least able to be assessed in the show ring; therefore judges' decisions play a very minor part in ensuring that the characteristics of the breed are maintained. The responsibility thus falls on the breeders to keep the Border Collie's reputation intact for future generations. If we are not careful in our selection of stud dogs and whelping bitches and if we are not honest with ourselves or our colleagues then many of the dog's desirable characteristics will be lost to the breed. It seems to me that sometimes breeders remember every section of the standard except the section headed characteristics.

Guidelines for assessing your dog's characteristics might include:

• Intelligence—bright, alert, interested in what is happening, keen to check out and investigate new places, sounds, etc., always ready for a game, chasing, jumping, fetching, able to master basic obedience, responds quickly to being called, told to sit, and so on.

• Instinct to work—when not under direct control, does the dog instinctively herd children or puppies, eye flies, chase-up birds, creep up on the cat or whatever, pounce on a stray leaf blowing across the lawn, crouch.

• Alertness—should be found in the whole demeanour of the dog: to be alert means virtually being on your guard; keen and ready to respond to whatever might happen next. It means the dog has a number of its senses working at once.

Its ears are listening, indicated by lifting and moving. (A word of caution here: ears which are simply semi-erect are not necessarily indicating alertness, no more than is a head swinging from side to side in response to a food stimulus.)

Its olfactory system (nose et al) is reading the scents, possibly indicated by the slight quiver or lift of the nose.

Eyes are watching.

Muscles are flexed and ready.

The dog is 'standing high'.

• Loyalty and faithfulness—in my opinion a beautiful characteristic of the Border Collie and one which should be carefully guarded. Is your dog happy to be with you, watchful when you are out of sight, will he sound a warning at an approaching stranger or someone unknown attempting to borrow your property? When running free with you does he keep coming back to see where you are, perhaps circling you occasionally? When unrestricted on his own territory does he stay around and look after things? (A note of caution: Loyalty may start out as instinctive in the dog but it is developed and maintained as a result of love and trust between dog and owner.)

• Kindly disposed towards stock—although we can't truly judge this characteristic unless we confront the dog with stock, nevertheless this disposition is one aspect that both breeders and judges must keep well in hand. The Border Collie should be neither aggressive nor a biter; this is obvious when we remember that he was selectively bred to use with sheep because he did not bite, nor for that matter, bark unduly. Therefore, a well adjusted Border Collie should not be known as a biter, neither should he be openly aggressive towards other dogs except when provoked, guarding or put-off by a bitch in season. My experience has been that a Border Collie, when confronting the household cat, for example, will only attempt to chase, pounce or 'set'! If introduced correctly to fowls, the Border Collie should be quite trustworthy. At one period I had three Border Collies, a pet rabbit and a cat all living in my backyard. The rabbit slept cuddled up to my old Border Collie bitch! Border Collies are renowned for being good with children. No matter how desirable are the other aspects of a particular animal considered for use in breeding, nothing should come before good temperament. Furthermore, as the standard indicates, 'any aspect of structure or temperament foreign to a working dog is uncharacteristic'. Our dogs should be judged on *all* requirements of the standard, including 'characteristics'. Thus, if a dog is lacking in intelligence or good sense,

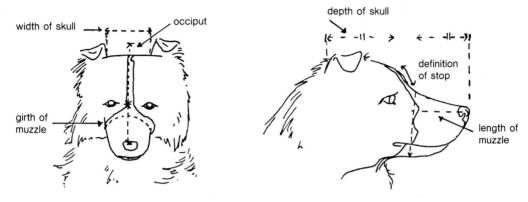

Head measurement planes

Both heads show well defined stop, good length of muzzle and strong underjaw. Note the effect of differing ear carriage and markings

is dull and disinterested, shows no working instincts or is of dubious or unsound temperament, then it is not adhering to the requirements of the standard.

3. Head

Key words: Broad, flat between the ears, pronounced stop, muzzle the same length as the skull, nose pigment

Faults: None specified

Comments: The head dimensions are taken: across the top of the head between the ears, from the mid-point of this imaginary line to the start of the stop, from the base of the stop to the end of the nose (i.e. the length of the muzzle), the girth of the muzzle and the angle of the stop (see diagram).

The skull is required to be flat between the ears. This is easily determined by placing the flat of the hand between the ears; there should be no feeling of roundness or dominess nor any ridges discernible. The breadth or distance between the ears is described as 'broad'; this does not mean excessively wide, but the relationship between this distance, and the length of the skull and the length of the muzzle should give approximately the proportions 1⅓:1:1. (*Note:* these are ratios, not actual measurements.) The muzzle itself should be thick and the bottom jaw quite strong; as a rule of thumb the girth of the muzzle just below the cheeks should be approximately treble its length.

The stop is that part of the dog's face which starts approximately between the eyes and slopes down to the start of the muzzle. It is very characteristic of a Border Collie head that a clearly definable angle is formed at the base of the stop, most clearly seen when looking at the head side on. The stop should not merge imperceptibly into the dog's profile.

Overall the head dimensions should give the appearance of symmetry and of great strength. Although no faults are specified in the standard, it is generally accepted that the head of the Border Collie should not appear 'snipey' or fox-like, as might occur if the muzzle was longer than the length of skull or if the breadth of skull (between the ears) was narrow or domey or if the girth of the muzzle was too thin or the face lacked stop. (As we shall see later, eye and ear expression have a bearing on this as well.) Neither should the head appear 'blocky' or 'thick', as might happen if the breadth of skull were excessive, or the muzzle too short relative to the length of skull or the stop were too exaggerated.
• 'Clean-cut', 'refined' and 'strong' are words often used in reference to a Border Collie's head.
• Nose pigment—unfortunately nose pigment is not as clearly defined as it could be in the standard. But with due regard to the genetics of colour, the nose pigment should be black in black, tricolour and the majority of red-coated dogs (it is possible, but very uncommon, for a red dog to have a liver nose); the nose pigment should be liver in chocolate-coated dogs (never black) and slate-grey in blue dogs. It is preferable that the nose be completely pigmented, that is, that there are no pink patches showing. (The seriousness of lack of pigment is relevant to the dog's appearance as a whole, but keep in mind that a dog can suffer very nasty sunburn on unpigmented areas of the nose.)

4. Eyes

Key words: Set wide apart, oval shape, moderate size, harmonise with the coat colour, typify expression

Faults: None specified

Comments: The standard here is reasonably self-explanatory. There are just two points that I would like to touch on.
• Eye colour—eye colour is affected by relevant genes or alleles in a similar manner to nose pigment, thus the main coat colour has a bearing on the eye colour. In black, tricolour and the majority of reds, a dark brown eye is possible and preferred. In chocolate and blue-coated dogs, a dark eye is simply not possible genetically, so a lightish or amber eye is correct.

The appearance of one blue eye (with one brown eye) is fairly common among Border Collies, with references to a 'wall' or 'blue' eye being found in the very early literature. While presenting no real problem to a working dog, the wall eye is not permissible in a show ring. Care should be exercised when breeding with known wall-eye carriers as this is a genetically heritable characteristic.
• Eyes as an indicator of expression—the eyes show if the dog is alert, keen, interested in its surroundings and sweet natured and intelligent. Thus a Border Collie's eyes should never be 'vacant', 'staring' or 'piggy' in appearance. Eyes which could be described as 'beady', or too small or roundish in shape, may cause the dog to take on a fox-like appearance. Also, the eyes contribute greatly to the soft and intelligent expression of a Border Collie. Hard eyes should not be encouraged.

Again, though no faults are specified, there is a tendency among Border Collies for some dogs' eyes to bulge or protrude; in my opinion this is undesirable and should be avoided.

5. Ears

Key words: Medium size, set well apart, carried semi-erect, sensitive in use, well furnished with hair inside

Faults: None specified

Comments: As already alluded to, the standard—correct in as far as it goes—falls short of reality when it comes to the Border Collie and its ears. Semi-erect ears, though they may be the preference of some Border Collie fanciers (not necessarily the majority), are

Chocolate tricolour puppy at four weeks. Tan is clearly discernible on eyebrows, cheeks and legs even in the chocolates

Litter brother and sister showing dark and light chocolate. Note that the ears on the bitch in the foreground were pricked by nine months

Black and chocolate puppies from the same litter showing that at five weeks eyes may still be baby blue

The all-round Border Collie takes showing, obedience trialling and sheep work all in his stride

Ticking clearly visible on muzzle
and front legs is also found in
collar

Top right: A puppy's ears will
often change during teething

Right: but come good in the adult
dog

Even at four weeks of
age this puppy is
showing potential for
good movement—
length of reach in
front, head inclined,
level topline and
strong hindquarters

Left: old style rose ear; right: semi-erect ear set to the side

certainly not the only type of ear carriage to be found in the genetic background of the modern Border Collie. A soft 'rose' ear figures prominently in many of our champion dogs of the past. Furthermore, there is a great deal of disagreement between judges, breeders and fanciers as to what is meant by a 'semi-erect' ear and what is meant by a 'rose' ear*, and whether 'heavy' ears should also be a part of the standard. (In fact the English standard permits a pricked ear.)

The way the ears look is the result of four factors: the set-on of the ear, the break-point of the ear-flap, the size and shape of the ear-flap or lobe, and the ability of the ear to move and lift (see page 93).

• The set-on of the ear—refers to the position of the junction between the ear lobe and the skull, with the reference point being the eyes. The ears may be set-on 'high', i.e. joining the skull above eye-level; or set-on low, i.e. joining the skull below eye-level. They may be positioned facing the front or slightly turned to the side.

In the Border Collie all four positions are found, though the ear-set somewhere in between 'high' and 'low' and turned slightly to the side would appear to have been the most favoured in the past.

• The break-point—refers to that part of the ear lobe where the ear folds or turns over. This could occur anywhere from the base of the ear to just the very tip of the ear or anywhere in between. I feel that the use of the word 'semi' in regards to the Border Collie ear is inappropriate, as I feel it is causing breeders to incorrectly emulate the semi-erect ear as found in the Collie Rough, where the standard defines semi-erect as '2/3 standing and 1/3 tipping forward'. This wording is not part of the Border Collie standard.

• Size—self-explanatory; generally a medium-sized ear with a blunted triangular shape is most acceptable.

• Lift—as already indicated, it is an essential characteristic of the Border Collie as a working dog that his sense of hearing should be constantly tuned in; the reference to ear movement is of great significance. When the dog is moving well stretched out his ears are normally laid back; when relaxed or sleeping the ears normally fall softly over the orifice; in both cases any unusual sound or verbal contact should bring them up and moving in the direction of the sound. It should be noted that it is the ear moving (and not the ear break-point) which is part of the dog's expression of alertness.

---

*Though the rose ear is part of the standard history of the Border Collie I wonder whether a mistake in terminology has occurred as I have never seen a Border Collie with the ear set shown under 'rose ear' in the book *Canine Terminology* by Dr H. Spira. Instead, I believe that what has been loosely called a rose ear in the past has been a medium set ear turned slightly to the side of the head and with a very low breakpoint. When this type of ear, which is very common, is laid back it would give the impression of a rose style ear.

6. Mouth

Key words: Teeth sound, strong, scissor bite

Faults: None specified

Comments: The standard is quite specific requiring strong sound teeth occurring in a scissor bite. There should be 42 teeth present in the dog's mouth and though it is understandable that occasionally a dog will lose a tooth accidentally, it should also be noted that some dogs do not develop a full complement of teeth by adulthood, occasionally missing pre-molars. The lower jaw of the Border Collie should be strong and sound, showing no tendency to recede, thus ensuring a good scissor bite.

Though no faults are specified, to have a scissor bite requires that the jaw is not:
• Undershot—that is, the lower jaw protrudes beyond the upper jaw.
• Overshot—where the top jaw, hence teeth, protrude beyond the lower, so that they do not come together correctly. This is usually the result of a small or receding lower jaw.
• Pincer-like—which occurs when the cutting surfaces of the front teeth meet together.

7. Neck

Key words: Good length, strong, muscular, slightly arched, broadening to the shoulders

Faults: Throatiness, coarseness

Comments: A correct length of neck is important in a Border Collie as outwardly it gives the dog its balanced, well proportioned appearance and its look of gracefulness and quality, especially in movement. More importantly, though, the neck (and head) are responsible for shifting the centre of gravity as the dog is moving, thus enabling the animal to adjust to changes in speed and power. Furthermore, the muscles of the upper arm are attached to the vertebrae which form the base of the neck and movement of the neck exerts an influence on the direction of pull of these muscles (see Movement, pages 81–82). Thus a shortened neck reduces available muscle support which in turn results in a shortened forward reach. Dimensions cannot be given but overall the dog should 'look right'. A long swan-like neck is not

correct; neither should the dog look as though its head is sitting on its shoulders!

'Throatiness' refers to a lack of firmness in the neck, i.e. a degree of looseness in the skin under the throat.

'Coarseness' means a thick, clumsy appearance to the neck.

Finally, an attractive appearance results from the neck broadening out gracefully to the set-on at the shoulders.

8. Forequarters

Key words: Shoulders long, well angulated, forelegs well boned, straight and parallel, pasterns flexible and slightly sloped

Faults: Elbows in or out

Comments: For explanations of angulation and bone see Terminology, page 63. The correct angulation, the angle formed by the points A, B & C in the diagram (which are chosen because they are able to be felt externally), is normally given as approximately 90°. When the dog is standing correctly (see Stance below) the placement of the shoulder to provide this angulation is significant and is referred to as shoulders well-laid back. The purpose here is to achieve the forequarter assembly which enables the dog to cover ground in the most energy efficient manner.

The length of the shoulder blades and humerus should be at least equal, with a good length required in the upper arm to give the dog maximum reach with its front legs and extra length of muscle. A short upper arm should not be encouraged as it reduces the dog's ability to reach and cover ground with a minimum of effort.

To achieve correct movement the forequarters must be complemented by the hindquarters.

When looking at the dog from the front, the front legs should be straight, parallel to each other and correctly positioned in relation to the breadth of the chest; again a function of the correct lay of the shoulder relative to the ribcage.

As a rough guide an average sized adult hand should fit snugly between the ribcage and the upper leg. An over-sprung or barrelled ribcage can cause the dog to be out at shoulder while a flat ribcage or upright shoulder blade causes the upper arms to be too close together, described as 'close in front'.

Looking at the dog side on should show the pasterns

Photo by T. Dorizas

A well angulated dog showing a good length of body

Left: Desirable shoulder angulation

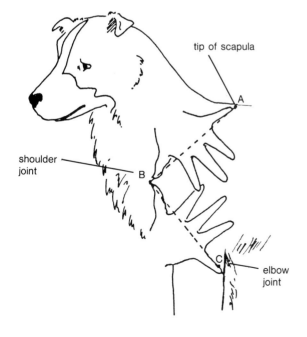

sloping slighty forwards. This, combined with their flexibility, is essential to cushion the shock as the dog's feet hit the ground in working gait.

• Stance—to make a correct assessment of the forequarters, the dog must be standing correctly. This is achieved by placing the heel pad directly in line with a point in the centre of the shoulder blade; looking down onto the dog over the shoulder the feet only should be visible.

• Elbows—the front legs should be parallel so that neither the elbows nor the shoulders go in or out. Thus looking at the dog from the front the legs should not appear to form a bow nor should the elbows turn in towards the chest.

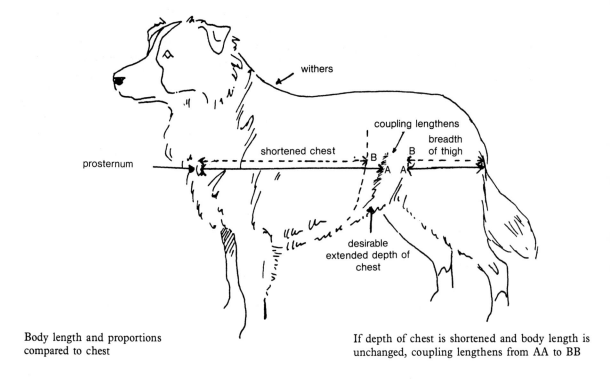

Body length and proportions compared to chest

If depth of chest is shortened and body length is unchanged, coupling lengthens from AA to BB

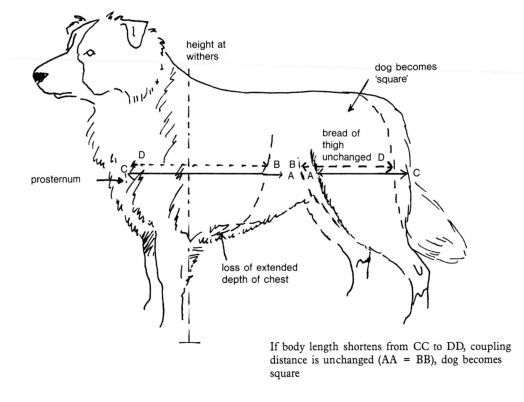

If body length shortens from CC to DD, coupling distance is unchanged (AA = BB), dog becomes square

9. Body

Key words: Moderately long, ribs well sprung, chest deep, moderately broad, loins broad, muscular, only slightly arched, flanks deep

Faults: Flank cut up

Comments: The body measurement is taken with reference to the dog's height. The Standard specifies that the body should be 'moderately long', i.e. the length of the body should be greater than the dog's height. This implies that the dog should not appear 'square' in proportions. Opinions differ as to whether the reference points are from the furthermost points of the buttocks to the pro-sternum or the point of the shoulder. This could result in a considerable difference in the ratio of length to height if:

  i) the dog has an exaggerated pro-sternum
  ii) the dog has an upright shoulder
  iii) the dog has an overangulated shoulder

   It seems to me that actual body length is secondary to the desired conformation of the dog giving good, sound endurance movement. Thus, the depth of chest needs to be maintained along the length of chest. A close look at the construction of a dog's body length shows that it is made up of three parts—the length of chest, the coupling, and the breadth of the thighs.

   These are all interrelated and contribute to the correct conformation of the dog. The Border Collie's ability to work untiringly is a function of its chest capacity. The chest capacity is defined by the length of the chest as well as the depth of the chest. Lung expansion takes place deep into the chest towards the abdominal wall. The heart also is housed within the thoracic cavity. Thus, the depth of chest should be maintained to a vertical imaginary line taken from the lowest point of the back down the line of the 9th rib to the brisket line.* If the actual length of the chest is shortened, depth of chest is lost and a tucked-up appearance results. As a result the dog either shortens into undesirable 'square' proportions, or the coupling lengthens, introducing the possibility of weakness in the back.

   The ribs, of course, are important in that they define the dimensions of the ribcage and thus chest capacity. 'Well-sprung' refers to the curvature of the rib bones away from the vertebral column. The ribs should not arch out too close to the vertebral column as this will impede the dog's movement, the chest becoming too rounded and wide. The other extreme is 'flat-ribbed', which will result in a narrow chest; thus the front legs are too close together and the chest capacity is reduced.

   The complete outline of the dog is complemented by clean-cut, slightly arched flanks and loins, which should be sufficiently well muscled to add strength to the hindquarters. The lower outline from the end of the length of chest should merge gracefully into the slight arching of the flank. If the curve rises too sharply ('cuts-up'), the hindquarters assembly loses strength and fluidity.

10. Hindquarters

Key words:
Croup—broad, muscular, slope to tail-set;
thighs—long, broad, deep, muscular;
stifles—well turned; hocks—strong, well let down, straight and parallel

Faults: Stiltiness, cow-hocks, bow-hocks

Comments: While the forequarter assembly provides reach and fulfils the function of weight-bearing, the hindquarters provide the drive and thrust required for locomotion, i.e. the dog propels itself forward with its back legs, and ensures maximum distance will be covered with each drive by the reach of its front legs. With this in mind it becomes clear why the front and rear quarters must complement each other. Additional considerations include the ability to turn suddenly and quickly and endurance (as opposed to speed).

   It is important to remember that the hindquarters are not primarily the profusion of coat and feathering we see when we look at a dog, but are a combination of muscles, bones and tendons, each with a specific task to accomplish in relation to each other for correct movement.

   Firstly, the muscles forming the croup should be broad and strong. When viewed from the top, the dog should not appear to narrow-in from the withers to the rump.

   Underlying the muscles of the croup is the pelvis. The slope of this bone from where it is attached to the sacrum to where it is anchored to the femur or top of the leg is crucial to the overall correct structure of the hindquarters. A reference to angles is often made to indicate a correctly sloped pelvic bone, but this angulation is extremely difficult to determine in a live

---

*McDowell-Lyons, *The Dog in Action*

This dog shows angulation, substance and strength

Photo by Michael M. Trafford

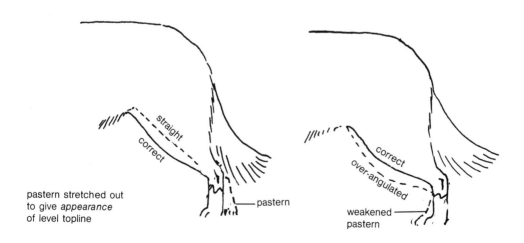

pastern stretched out
to give *appearance*
of level topline

pastern

weakened
pastern

Turn of stifle: straight stifle and over-angulated stifle compared to the desirable conformation dog. A well shaped pelvis will appear externally as a croup sloping downwards to the set of the tail and a well turned stifle joint.

The turn of stifle is best (though not accurately) viewed as the whole curvature of the dog's leg from the hock to the buttocks. This should appear as a gradual easy curve, neither exaggerated nor straight (see page 78).

The thigh muscles should be both broad and long, while a similar length is also required in the lower leg bones (tibia and fibula) as this provides extra length for the Achilles tendon and muscle.

If the rear assembly is to stay balanced with the rest of the dog, the extra length desirable in the tibia and fibula is achieved by a shortening of the bones of the rear pastern, thus the hocks must be well let down. In other words, the closer the hock to the ground (relatively) the greater the length available for the development of the Achilles tendon and muscle, so crucial to movement.

The pasterns should be strong, well boned and straight. It is the action of the Achilles tendon on the hock joint which straightens the leg and provides leverage to propel the body forward. The hocks should not slope towards the front of the dog, as would result from an over angulated stifle.

Although no faults are specified in this section, I believe the following departures from the requirements of the standard should be recognised:
• Croup too flat—this results in a lack of slope from the croup and thus a high tail-set. Although the flatter croup may enable the leg to extend further rearwards, it restricts the dog's ability to turn on its hindquarters. The ability to turn instantly while moving is an essential requirement to a working Border Collie and therfore we should breed to retain this characteristic. A well sloped croup enables the dog to get to his feet quickly underneath himself and then turn on his hindquarters, rather than having to move in a circle from the front.*
• Straight stifle—appears as the leg being too upright and often results in a 'bum-high' appearance, i.e. the area of the top line from the rump to the croup is higher than the topline to the front of the rump when the dog is moving. A straight stifle results in a stilted, choppy gait which lacks drive and restricts endurance, requiring excessive energy to maintain movement.
• Cow-hocks and bow-hocks—when the dog is viewed from behind and in a standing position his legs should appear parallel and the pasterns straight. The hocks should not turn in (cow-hocks) neither should the whole leg bow out (bow-hocks).

*McDowell-Lyons, *The Dog in Action*

11. Feet

Key words: Oval shaped; pads deep, strong, sound; toes moderately arched, close together

Faults: None specified

Comments: The feet are a crucial part of the equipment of the dog—indeed, his stamina for working is only as good as his feet. The Border Collie's feet should be oval in shape, compact and of a size to complement the rest of the dog. The feet should not splay out when supporting the dog's weight in a standing position. Thus, he should be well up on his toes. The pads bear the brunt of running on rough ground, stones and hard roads; when the dog is gaiting the heel pads hit the ground first and must be able to absorb the initial shock and withstand the impact of the ground. Thus, the leathers should be deep, tough and well pigmented and not given to splitting. The depth of the pads is roughly measured by one finger joint.

12. Tail

Key words: Set-on low, moderately long, upward swirl at the end

Faults: Carried over the back

Comments: It is often the case that the tail of the Border Collie is dismissed or overlooked. Personally, I consider this is a fundamental error, as the tail can indicate a great deal about the animal. The tail completes the balance of the dog, not only in appearance, but in movement. By 'moderately long' is taken to mean reaching to the hock joint when held straight down. The balanced appearance of the Border Collie is enhanced by a well-feathered tail which curves gracefully downwards and slightly upwards at the end.

A low set-on tail is called for. This indicates a well sloped pelvis as discussed in the section on Hindquarters. A tail which comes straight out from the topline is incorrect and indicates a too-flat slope to the pelvic bone. On the other hand, the tail-set should not be so low as to cause the tail to hang between the back legs, beneath the dog's body.

The tail is an essential part of the dog's movement and body language and much can be gleaned about muscular development and attachments from the dog's tail. A tail which is held to one side, for example, is usually an indication of weakness in one or more of the muscles along the spinal column. The thickness of the vertebrae at the base of the tail gives an indication of the width and strength of the vertebrae along the spinal column. A good width and projection is desirable for the strong attachment of muscles.

The specified fault is a tail carried over the back, known as a 'gay tail'. This is usually the result of a tail set too high, which in turn indicates incorrect slope of the pelvic bone and a possible weakness of one or more of the rear muscles. There is an increasing tendency to overlook this fault as a flattened croup can still be accompanied by an adequate turn of stifle and therefore the appearance of reasonable movement can be maintained, especially if the dog has a compensating fault in the front assembly. However, a well sloped croup firstly enables the Border Collie to turn quickly while moving and secondly is compatible with the ability to move in an energy efficient manner leading to endurance, two characteristics which cannot be ascertained in the show ring and therefore must be all the more closely watched through anatomical detail. (Great speed is not required in a working sheepdog, but endurance is.)

13. Movement

Key words: Free, smooth, tireless, minimum lift of feet, straightforward and true, strength and flexibility

Faults: Weakness at shoulders, elbows, pasterns, stiltiness, cow-hocks, bow-hocks

Comments: It is not possible here to do full justice to this aspect of the Standard's requirements. Many books have been written about movement alone and the interested reader is referred to a study of these.

I believe movement in a Border Collie to be of prime importance. A Border Collie in full flight is a beautiful sight; a Border Collie 'clapping', 'creeping' and turning is an equally riveting sight. Any Border Collie owner who has not seen this side of their dog's ability is missing not only something very pleasurable, but also the whole point of this animal as a working dog! A working Border Collie *is* movement! If we allow ourselves to breed dogs incapable of correctly carrying out this function, then we are destroying the essence of this breed. To my mind, the Border Collie should be built for endurance and flexibility before speed, as correct movement is the most energy efficient movement. All of the body parts of a dog are involved either directly or indirectly in movement; therefore, how a dog moves can tell the observer much about both the visible and not directly visible parts of the dog's anatomy.

Desirable movement
To do his task correctly the Border Collie will gallop, trot, walk, 'creep', 'clapp' and turn. These are defined as follows:

• Gallop—the movement employed by the dog when running free and stretching out. It is a four-beat movement, meaning that each foot takes off and hits the ground at different times, but in sequence. As the dog gains momentum he appears to bound over the ground, and a period of suspension occurs when the dog actually has all four feet off the ground. This is considered the fastest action of the dog. The power of the gallop is derived from the straightening of the back legs; a function of correct angulation and strong rear muscles.

• Trot—the medium paced endurance movement employed by the dog. It is a two-time movement, with the front and rear legs moving in sequence on the diagonal and with this sequence the body is always supported. A working dog uses the trot to cover rough ground and long distances. Knowledge of the trot is of special concern to Show exhibitors as it is the movement the judge requires when the request to 'Gait round the ring' is made. This movement shows the dog to its best advantage in terms of conformation, angulation and balance.

• Walk—a slow movement employed for easy travelling. It involves a four-time movement in which the legs move one after the other diagonally. As the body is always supported by three legs during a walk it is considered the least tiring method of progression.

• Creep—an exaggerated slow movement peculiar to the Border Collie. To accomplish this movement, the dog lowers the front-half of its body and keeping his lead low but parallel to the ground, moves stealthily forward, carefully placing one foot after the other. This movement, so necessary for the gentle but firm control of sheep, is often accompanied by eye control.

• Clapp—the ability to drop to the crouch position instantly; also useful for the control of flocks.

• Turn—the ability to change direction, ostensibly in mid-air, by getting the hind-feet under the body as it swings around into the opposite direction. This avoids the need for a wide circle of movement as would occur if the hind-legs had to follow the front legs around on the ground. This is a function of a well-sloped croup.

The mechanics of correct movement

The Standard specifies that the movement of a Border Collie be 'free, smooth and tireless, with a minimum lift of the feet', also straightforward and true; overall conveying the impression to 'move with great stealth'. This type of movement does not occur accidentally; nor can a dog be trained to move correctly. Correct movement comes from a correctly conformed and angulated dog, backed up by muscle tone.

Conformation—refers to the orderly arrangement of the parts of the dog; for the show Border Collie this means representing the requirements of the Standard. As the Standard was drawn up originally to ensure that the breed remains functionally correct ('capable of enduring long periods of active duty in its intended task as a working sheep dog'), it seems to me that conformation must be judged in the stationary and moving positions. (*Note:* A correctly conformed dog will be a well balanced dog but the reverse does not necessarily follow.)

• Angulation—conformation embodies the correct angulation required for soundness and movement as well. By angulation is meant the angles formed by various bones of the skeletal system relative to what is considered desirable for a given function. For our present consideration this means lay of shoulder, upper to lower arm, slope to pelvic bone, turn of stifle, pasterns, front and rear.

• Muscular system—initially it is the contraction or expansion of the muscles which moves the skeletal system, while the length and placement of various bones and width of certain protrusions determines the correct length of and strong attachments of the muscles. The muscles should be well developed, well toned and strong. This does not mean they should be over-developed or bulgy in appearance; as with a correctly angulated dog, this is unnecessary for correct movement. Over-development of the muscles will cause the dog to lose its graceful appearance and, depending on which muscles are over-developed, make the dog look bossy in front or bulgy in the rear. Over-developed thigh muscle usually results from an attempt to correct a weakness in the hindquarters.

• Feet and head—these two parts of the dog are often overlooked in their relative importance to the dog's movement ability. A little commonsense will show how unwise this is. Even the most correctly put together dog will only move correctly as long as his feet can sustain him. Tough, thick, horny pads do not break gait when they strike a bindii or a patch of rough ground or prickly grass. Obviously the feet strike the ground first and thus must be able to cushion the initial shock before it is dispersed through the pastern to the muscles.

The length of neck and head affects the dog's centre of gravity and it is continually adjusted by the dog to maintain equilibrium.

• Chest dimensions—affect the movement of the dog in two important ways: the structure of the rib-cage affects the lay-of-shoulder, thus foreleg placement, and the length and depth of the chest defines heart and lung capacity, thus stamina and endurance.

Gait

Movement is essentially the result of the body ascending and descending. Correct movement is energy efficient, enabling the dog to sustain endurance over time and balance. It is the outcome of the following mechanical actions:

• Reach—the extending of the front leg forwards. How the dog can reach determines its ability to cover ground.

• Lift and drive—the contractions of the rear muscles and the Achilles tendon straightens the hock, resulting in the dog 'driving off' with its back leg. The power of this thrust depends upon the length of the back leg when fully extended.

• A shift in the centre of gravity—according to McDowell-Lyons, 'the flatter the arc transcribed by the rise and fall of the centre of gravity, the less energy needed to move across it'. Basically, this means the less the dog's body curves between the front and back assemblies with each stride, the less energy is needed to take the dog forwards. You can test this out in a simple way yourself: walk a given distance with a normal stride, then walk the same distance pushing yourself upwards with the back foot each time. Notice when you push up how your stride is shortened, requiring more steps to cover the same distance, how difficult it becomes to maintain your balance, and how long you can/cannot keep up walking in this fashion.

'A minimum lift of the feet' in the moving dog is outwardly observed by the rise and fall of the withers.

• Side-to-side swing—as the dog moves diagonally from right-front leg to left-back leg, then left-front leg to right-rear leg, the body is continually shifting sideway back and forth. As speed increases the dog will adjust to this movement by inclining the leg further in towards the centre, thus giving the body more support and maintaining balance along the midline.

• Adjustment of the head and neck—at leisure pace, walking or ambling a Border Collie will hold its head up (but not backwards of its shoulders); at working gait the head drops in line with the body, the neck stretches forwards. The reason for this is that the dog is moving the weight off the back of the body and onto the front of the body (by altering the centre of gravity), thus allowing the hindquarters to exert more power and increase speed. The inclined head and neck lowers wind resistance. A sudden stop will see the head go up to assist in braking.

It should be clear from all of this that the front and back of the dog should complement each other. If the angulation of the dog falters at both ends, but in a compensating manner, then at least the dog can still move true within its own limits and present a picture of balanced action. By and large (though not always) movement faults occur when the front and rear quarters are mismatched in some way.

Movement faults

• Breaking gait—appears as 'bunny-hopping' in the hind legs. This may result from the stifle being too straight and unable to match the reach of the front legs. The dog resorts to a half gallop to keep pace. Other factors may also cause the dog to break gait, e.g. lack of muscle development or the handler attempting to trot the dog too quickly.

• Crabbing—describes the dog which moves with its hindquarters to the side of its front, i.e. it does not run straight. Crabbing is usually the result of a reach too short for the drive, so that the dog's back feet would clip the front feet as they come together. To avoid this (which would cause the dog to stumble) the dog learns to reach its back feet past its front feet and to the side of them, thus continually swinging its body sideways. Crabbing can also be seen in a dog which is too short in coupling.

• Stiltiness—a choppy, stiff-legged movement, particularly in the back legs, which appears to lack 'stride'. This is usually the outcome of poor front angulation, which the dog compensates for by shortening the rear leg action into a 'lift' of the hindquarters. The backline does not appear level as the dog moves, but the line of the croup rises and falls above the line of the mid-back. Thus the dog is expending energy going up and down rather than forwards and lacks endurance.

• 'Piston-like' movement—usually the result of a lack of angulation in the front. A too-straight shoulder reduces the dog's ability to reach forwards, so that the legs appear to move more up than out. Often this type of movement is very fast, but because the dog is not covering ground, it uses up a greater amount of energy than a correctly angulated dog would to cover the same distance. A short upper arm may also restrict reach.

• Paddling—appears as a dog 'flicking' his front feet upwards or sideways before striking the ground. This requires extra muscle movement which becomes energy-wasteful. Again, paddling is usually a compensation action for a fault elsewhere, usually a lack of reach associated with a lack of complementary angulation between the front and rear. If the force of the drive pushes the dog further than its ability to reach, the animal must find a way to delay its front feet hitting the ground too soon and losing its balance; flicking the feet upwards is the one means of delaying their striking the ground. Another way of achieving a semblance of balance between incompatible front and rear assemblies is for the dog to shorten its rear drive.

• The faults as listed in the standard—cow-hocks, bow-hocks, out at shoulder or elbows, or weak or incorrectly angulated pasterns (all of which have been described elsewhere)—will interfere with correct movement in numerous ways. Probably the best way to recognise these problems is to first carefully study the gait of a correctly conformed dog (or as close to correct as you can find) and then compare it to the movement of one with any of the above faults.

Cow-hocks restrict the dog's ability to move true, i.e. for the hind-legs to follow the front in a straight line, the dog will run with the appearance of the legs dangling to the side. Bow-hocks limit the ability of the leg to straighten and this restricts the power of the drive.

Weakness at shoulder or elbow (looseness or weakness in the muscular attachments of the shoulder) cause the dog to cross-over its front legs and thus reduce its forward reach.

Weak pasterns refers to the slope of the pastern being either too straight or too oblique (slanted towards the ground) compared to the desirable slope. A straight pastern in the front will result in jarring as the pads hit the ground. Too much slope in the back pastern causes the dog's weight to be incorrectly distributed, resulting in a weak point reducing an endurance gait.

14. Coat

Key words: Double coated; top coat, weather resistant, moderately long, medium textured, dense; undercoat, short, soft, dense

Faults: None specified

Comments: The Standard is self-explanatory. The function of a Border Collie's coat is firstly to protect the dog from the weather, thus it should be 'weather resistant'. This results from both the denseness of the undercoat and the correct texture of the top coat. The top coat should not be soft to touch, neither dry nor coarse, but it should be such that it is very difficult to wet the dog to the skin. The outer coat should hold off moderate rain like an oilskin. A vigorous shake should result in the dog being almost dry. A good covering of short dense undercoat keeps the dog both warm and dry and I believe that a complete absence of undercoat should be considered a fault. It must be noted that as the dog sheds its coat, it takes on a somewhat bald appearance and will appear to lack undercoat at this time. The undercoat will usually begin to reappear in the area of the croup.

A Border Collie should not have an extreme profusion of coat. The coat is described as 'moderate' in length with extra length required around the neck and chest, along the inside legs and underside of the tail. The 'graceful outline' and 'balanced proportions' of the dog should always be evident and not obscured by excessive coat. To preserve the essentials of the Border Collie as a working dog the coat should be sufficient to provide the protection the dog needs but not such that it hinders functioning in the field. A long soft coat will pick up grass seeds and burrs and hold mud. A Border Collie with a correct length and texture of coat has no trouble in shaking himself clean.

Finally, the coat should preferably be straight, not inclined to waviness or curl.

Colour

The ancestry and genetic background of the Border Collie is such that a range of colours is possible. The Standard is specific on the individually acceptable colours, but makes no statement about the expression of those colours, which in fact do occur in a variety of shades.

The white pattern (markings) is also not specified but it is commonly accepted that the minimum would be four white feet, white chest and white tip to the tail. Markings vary and may include a full or part collar and a blaze along the centre of the face which may stop at a position between the eyes or extend over the top of the head; the white on the feet may extend to the hock on the back legs and to the elbow or further on the front legs. White markings on the body are not considered acceptable, but the remainder of the white markings are a matter of personal preference.

The tricolour pattern requires the usual minimum white markings with the addition of tan patches above the eyebrows, on the cheeks, and in a line between the white and the black on the legs. Tan may also occur under the tail.

Colour	Expression	Pigment	Eyes
Black	Dense, bluish chestnut— reddish tinge	Black	Brown
Blue (solid colour)	Steel grey 'Faded' black	Slate	Light brown
Chocolate (true brown)	Dark brown to light tan	Liver	Light brown to amber
Red	Pale wheaten to deep ginger (also described as cream, biscuit)	Black (usually)	Dark brown
Tricolour	Black with specific markings of rich tan shades	Black	Dark brown

15. Size

Dogs: 48–53 cm approx. (19–21 inches)
Bitches: 46–51 cm approx. (18–20 inches)

Requirements here are self-explanatory. However, care should be taken to ensure that at all times height, plus substance and conformation, result in an obvious difference between dogs and bitches. That is, the overall proportions of the dog should not result in a feminine or petite appearance while the bitches should not be allowed to become coarse or unfeminine in appearance. The actual height of the dog will play an important role in determining overall proportions.

16. Entirety

An adult male dog should be entire (two descended testicles). This may or may not be evident in a puppy, though it would be expected to become evident somewhere between the ages of six and nine months.

6 Genetics

Why genetics?

Breeders, exhibitors, in fact, dog people in general, are prone to uttering a continuous flow of observations such as 'Look at the heads on those pups; they got that from their father!', 'What magnificent angulation; that must come from Flossy's side', or 'One blue eye; I wonder where that comes from?'

Whether one is aware of it or not, all such remarks involve statements concerning genetic content. Genetics is defined as the study of the mechanism of heredity. It involves observation and investigation. When breeders move from simply observing—'Haven't they got good heads!' to asking 'why' questions—'Why did these pups get their father's head and not their mother's?'—they are opening up a pathway which, if pursued, should enable them to begin to predict rather than simply observe—'I should get good heads in this litter! but I shouldn't get blue eyes'. The result of this is greater control over the outcome of matings leading to a definable plan for breeding programs, ending up with 'the perfect dog'!

The science of inheritance is as old as living matter and just as dynamic. Evolution itself (the way a species has developed) is partly the result of selective breeding in nature and mutation (of the genetic material). Many of the findings of geneticists are neither exact nor immutable; generalisations are made, based on given data and observable results. Some characteristics may remain hidden in the animal's gene pool for many generations while their exact mode of inheritance, especially in dogs, is not known. This does not preclude an educated guess proving useful, but for Border Collie breeders the more information which can be gathered in a reliable fashion and shared the better able we would be to build up a body of useful knowledge regarding our breed.

One must also be aware of the actions of nature, environmental factors and chance; we should not fall into the trap of thinking we are in control for the genetic imprint from the parents only gives a puppy its start in life; to make the best of what is there depends upon the puppy's envrionment, which includes its owner, its feeding, exercise and accidental happenings.

The working language of genetics

A working knowledge of the language of genetics is helpful in understanding the basic concepts involved, but keep in mind that there is a vast depth of knowledge left untouched.

Following is a simplified list of the basic language employed in genetics. It must be pointed out that in attempting to simplify the meaning of the terms, a degree of accuracy is lost, but I believe that this list will still provide useful, workable knowledge for the majority of Border Collie breeders. Those who are interested are advised to read the specialised material; several references are included in the bibliography.

Terminology

Genetics   The study of the mechanism of heredity.
Autosomal inheritance   The transfer of characteristics which are not sex-linked.
Sex-linked   Characteristics which are transferred by

one sex only, but manifest in the opposite sex, e.g. haemophilia is carried by bitches but affects males.

Sex-limited   Characteristics which are carried by both male and female but which can only find expression in one sex, cryptorchidism (for the obvious reason that the bitch does not exhibit testicles).

Gene   The apparatus by which characteristics are transferred from parent to offspring. It is the pattern which the animal's cells will follow to develop. Functionally, genes appear in pairs.

Allele   Refers to each part of the pair of a gene which can result in differences in expression of the same characteristics.

Multiple allele series   The situation which arises when more than one alternative mutates from a given gene.

Heterozygous   A gene pair in which the two alleles are unalike.

Homozygous   A gene pair in which the two alleles are the same.

Phenotype   The expression of the dog's characteristics: appearance, nature.

Genotype   The genetic composition of a particular dog.

Polygenes   Groups of non-major genes which affect the expression of the characteristic of a major gene to a greater or lesser degree, e.g. red coat colour and the rufus group of polygenes.

Familial   A characteristic observed to occur in 'family' groupings of dogs but not proven to be heritable, e.g. poor eating patterns.

Inbreeding   Mating together closely related dogs, as in parent to offspring, brother to sister. This reduces the degree of random selection involved in the assortment of gene material, thus increasing homozygosity for a larger number of characteristics.

Linebreeding   A less intense form of inbreeding through which random selection is also reduced by consistently mating to a preferred animal or type of animal.

Grading-up   Improving one or a number of characteristics by repeatedly mating to better stock.

Linkage   The situation which arises when two genes on the same chromosome remain together during cell division. The characteristics manifested by these two genes always reappear together in the progeny.

Basic genetics

Autosomal inheritance

When a male and female gamete (egg and sperm cells) unite they will transfer certain of their sire's and dam's characteristics to the offspring. Both gametes carry a set of 39 matching chromosomes; when united this becomes 39 pairs or 78 chromosomes which is the normal chromosome count in a dog cell. (For interest, the chromosome count in human cells is 46.) The chromosomes are described as rod-like structures which carry the genes. It is the genes which provide the blueprint for the dog's cell structure to develop in a particular way. The genes also occur in pairs, one from each parent; each unit of the pair is known as an allele. The gene material, though forming a correct pair for cell division and thus growth to take place, may be made up of two alleles carrying different but compatible information. An easy way to visualise this is to think of a gene 'instructing' the production of pigment producing coat colour. One allele of the pair may be carrying the blueprint for the pigment to occur in such a way that the dog appears black, while its partner may carry the program for the pigment cells to form in such a way as to appear brown. Will the puppy end up black or brown? We know in this case (ignoring any other factors at this stage) that the puppy will be black. Thus we refer to the allele for black as being the dominant allele and the allele for brown as being recessive. The dominant allele is the one which always takes precedence over its partner.

Certain characteristics are known to be dominant, while others are known to be recessive (a limited coverage is given on pages 91–96). Border Collie people know that Border Collies are sometimes born brown. How does this happen? If the puppy receives a recessive brown allele from each parent (known as double recessive) it receives the 'message' to produce pigment cells in such a way that its coat appears brown (both alleles carry the same 'message').

The salient points so far are:
• Almost all aspects of the dog's make-up material is determined by both parents.
• Some characteristics are known (or assumed) to be dominant.
• For a recessive characteristic to show up both alleles of the gene for that characteristic must be recessive.

The gene material that the dog carries is known as the genotype for that dog. There are three possible genotype groupings for each characteristic. To continue with the coat colour example:

• A black puppy may have a coat colour gene with both alleles giving the message for black. This type is called 'double dominant'.

• A brown puppy must carry two alleles for brown; it can only pass on to its offspring the gene material for brown. This is commonly called 'double recessive' or 'homozygous recessive'.

• A second type of black puppy may carry one allele dominant for black and the other allele recessive for brown. This type of dog is capable of passing on either one of these to its offspring. This type is 'heterozygous'.

In the case of black coat colour as explained here it is not possible to determine simply by looking at the phenotype (the external appearance) whether the dog is homozygous dominant black or heterozygous black. Where a characteristic which is known to be a simple recessive appears it is almost always possible to determine its genotype from its phenotype, as in the example above of the brown coat. How then is it possible to determine the genotype of a dog manifesting a dominant characteristic?

In the simplest case, a puppy from a mating between a double recessive and phenotype dominant must be heterozygous, carrying both alleles for a particular characteristic. In the example above, this means that if a brown dog is mated to a black bitch (known not to be carrying any other colour) all the puppies will be black but will be carrying brown as well as black.

Another way is to gather information about the ancestry, siblings and progeny of related dogs and the dog in question. This may or may not provide a definitive answer.

The third way of determining a genotype is to conduct one or several test matings and keep records of the outcomes.

So far we have been dealing with a very simplified version of autosomal genetics and this should provide the novice in this field with a working knowledge for informed breeding. If the transfer of all the characteristics of our dogs were a simple case of 'two alternate allele' and now you see it, now you don't! then dog-breeding would be easy! But we all know that it isn't the case.

The dog is a 'picture' made up of many parts. Sometimes we are not aware of just how many. To take a simple example, we all know what a Border Collie's ear looks like; our main preoccupation is whether or nor the ear 'turns-over' in the right place! The break point of the ear is an heritable characteristic; but so is every other part of the ear—is the tip blunt or pointed, the base wide or narrow, the length of the ear lobe two inches or three inches, is the hair on the ear short or long, is the texture of the ear leather coarse or fine, is the placement to the front or the side, are both ears the same, and so on. Every one of these features of an ear is transferred from parents to offspring independently of each other. Multiply that by each individual part of the dog e.g. size, shape, colour, placement of the eye etc. and it becomes quite apparent that it is no mean feat to get it all right on the one dog!

Still, breeders are encouraged to become familiar with some of the laws of genetics for three simple reasons: firstly, the satisfaction gained from seeing an improvement in your dogs which you set out to achieve, secondly, to avoid breeding faults or undesirable abnormalities into the breed and lastly, to keep on adding to the genetic knowledge of the Border Collie.

When an egg is fertilised by a sperm following copulation, a process takes place which can be roughly summarised as follows:

1. The cells of a dog contain 78 chromosomes in 39 matching pairs.

2. Chromosomes are capable of producing an exact replica of themselves during cell division.

3. When cell division occurs to form germ-cells (gametes) in both males and females (i.e. sperm and egg cells), 39 chromosomes from each parent (that is, one from each matching pair) are carried forward to form the next generation.

4. Chromosomes carry the genes, which also occur in pairs; each individual member of that pair is called an allele. When the 39 chromosomes from each germ cell unite to form pairs, it is possible that the new pairings of genes will be compatible but not exactly the same. This outcome is known as the segregation and independent assortment of genes, and is the mechanism by which different manifestations of a characteristic occur.

Mutations

Mutation refers to a sudden change in the structure of a gene which results in a change in the expression of that gene; this changed gene is heritable (that is, able to be passed on to future generations). By and large the mutant allele is recessive to the original allele so that its presence remains hidden in the dog's gene pool until random selection causes mutant genes to align and thus reveal a different characteristic. The true recessive will breed true to its own type. Mutation is the means by which a breeding population 'evolves' or changes its form.

Causes of mutations

The cause of mutation comes mainly from the gene structure itself and may be the result of the gene material breaking and recombining or of the rearrangement of the gene material within itself. To date this has appeared to be a chance occurrence, with no common external causal factor having been isolated, though scientists have been attempting for many years to find ways of causing mutations. For our purposes, we cannot cause a mutation, but what we do do is breed for or against certain mutations to change the appearance of our dogs. Obviously these have to be characteristics which we can see in the phenotype or ones which we know exist in the gene material of the dog. Occasionally we are lucky (or sometimes unlucky) enough to throw up something which has not been encountered previously, but it should be stressed that mutations occur very infrequently. Sometimes a gene mutates to give rise to only one alternative of itself, e.g. the dilution gene 'D' and its counterpart 'd'–if 'D' is present a dog may have a black coat, while 'dd' changes the black coat to blue.

Allelic series

Geneticists have shown that sometimes, when the mutation is the result of the genetic material rearranging itself, it may give rise to a whole series of possible genetic variations, each one recessive to the one above it in the series. Even so, each dog will still only carry the normal number of alleles for one gene, i.e. two alleles, one from each parent. A common example of an allelic series in the dog is the so-called Agouti series which designates major coat colours in the following way:*

Black	A^s
Yellow	A^y
Agouti (wild grey)	A
Saddle pattern	a^s
Tan pattern	a^t

This series stretches well back into the evolution of the dog when each of the colours mutated from the

original wolf-grey of the dog's ancestors (agouti is a common colour pattern in wild animals—rats, rabbits, etc.). All solid colour patterns in the Border Collie, including tricolour, arise from this basic series of black or yellow pigment-carrying cells (the grey apparently having been selectively bred against and therefore lost to the Border Collie). The remaining colours (red, blue, brown) are the result of the actions of different sets of genes on the basic colours, black or yellow. At the same time, the depth of colour is the result of further modifier genes; much more work needs to be done before the full effect of modifier genes in the Border Collie is known.

Epistasis

This is one heritable effect of which the serious breeder should be aware. Epistasis refers to the situation where one gene 'hides' the outcome of another gene, as in the case of the recessive of the Extension gene (Ee) resulting in a dog appearing red/yellow. The dog could in fact be a dominant for black, a double recessive chocolate or a tricolour. Looking at the phenotype would give no indication, except in the case of the 'chocolate', in which case the red/yellow dog would have a liver coloured nose.

Sex determination

In the determination of a puppy's sexual characteristics (male or female) a slightly different set of circumstances occur to what we have been so far considering. Very simply, when cell division takes place, the eggs of the bitch all carry the female chromosome (designated X) but the spermatozoa of the male are split in such a way that half of the zygotes carry an X chromosome while the other half carry the chromosome for male characteristics, designated Y. Thus, as sperm and ova unite in random fashion during fertilisation, those eggs which are fertilised by an X-carrying sperm will, under normal circumstances, develop into females, while those receiving sperm carrying Y chromozomes will develop into males. Note that sex-linked characteristics are carried on the X and Y chromosomes.

Genetic ratios

Though breeders may give themselves a '1 in 2' or '1 in 4' chance of producing a certain characteristic in their puppies, it should be kept in mind that the population

---

*R. Robinson: *Genetics for Dog Breeders*

Mating between double recessives

sample on which such ratios are based are much larger than most breeders are prepared to produce. Very few breeders will continue to repeat matings a sufficient number of times or continue to keep records of the offspring to be able to build up an accurate picture of their inherited characteristics. Mostly we have to accept the predictions of those who have made a progressive study of the genetic ratios of the canine population.

Note, also, the effect of environmental factors and animal husbandry practises on the perceived results, e.g. puppies raised under adverse conditions may not achieve the expected height, weight, coat length etc.

Furthermore, care should be taken not to assume a characteristic to be dominant or recessive based on how often we see it in our stock. For example, in the Border Collie breed, ticking (p.94) is in fact a dominant characteristic although it is seen very rarely in our stock. This is the outcome of breeders selectively breeding for the recessive gene; either for personal preference or to satisfy the 'requirements' of the show ring.

It should be understood that continuous breeding for a recessive characteristic will eventually cause the dominant characteristic to be lost from the gene pool. For an animal to exhibit a recessive trait, e.g. the absence of ticking, it must have two recessive genes for that trait which precludes the possibility of carrying the dominant counterpart. To breed recessive males to recessive females means that none of the offspring will be capable of producing the dominant characteristic in their first generation of offspring. Clearly, this is not true when breeding for a dominant characteristic e.g. a black coat colour, since the dominant gene is capable of showing itself in the outward appearance whilst still allowing the pups to carry the recessive for example, a blue coat colour.

The most practical outcome of all of this is to be aware that while some characteristics can be easily recognised and controlled there are other parts of the dog for which either the exact mode of inheritance is not exactly known or for which the number of parts

Mating between heterozygous black
and double recessive chocolate

of expression are too many to be controllable. For example, it is relatively simple to breed together two animals having the genetic material capable of producing a given colour, say blue, but the depth or lightness of that blue is not so simple to achieve. On the other hand, commonsense tells us that a dog's height, for example, must be governed by many genes, viz. the separate length of each of the bones in the legs, or the body for a start. And yet in the main, breeders manage to stay within a 5 centimetre variation for the height of a vast number of Border Collies!

Averaging the population

Without really knowing how to shorten a femur or lengthen a tibia, standard heights can be maintained, as indeed can numerous other multi-mixed characteristics. Breeders can do this quite naturally by a combination of the following procedures:

1. Avoid mating extremes of phenotype, e.g. prick-eared dog to a heavy-eared bitch does not ensure puppies with semi-erect ears, simply some with pricked ears and some with heavy ears, unless both extremes are carrying the genetic material to produce semi-erect ears.

2. Select and cull with the population average in mind, e.g. if ear carriage is under consideration, discarding pricked eared or extremely heavy-eared dogs will allow the breeding population to increase the number of animals with semi-erect ears. In this way the whole of a given population can move towards the desired condition or population average; if each generation consistently eliminates undesirable extremes, the nature of random selection has more chance of reproducing to the average. (This does not mean that the possibility of the extremes is totally eliminated, only that the odds of producing an extreme are reduced.)

3. A useful rule of thumb among dog breeders is that if a particular animal is a desirable type, then look to the parents of that animal for use in your breeding

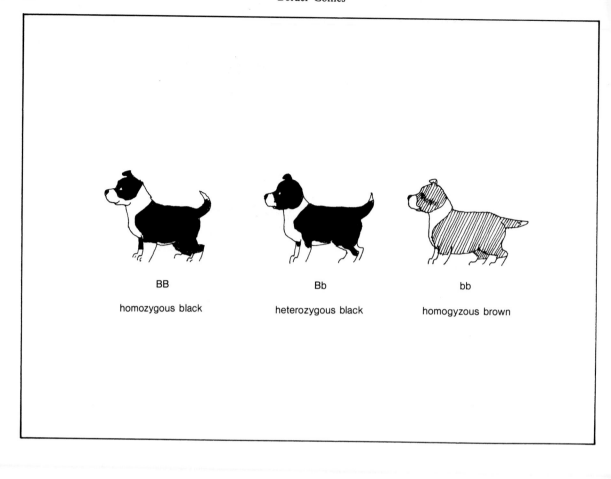

BB   Bb   bb

homozygous black   heterozygous black   homogyzous brown

program; you have more chance of gaining the gene characteristics of a given type from the sire than from the dog himself.

4. Recognise that nature plays a part in population selection. Put simply, factors operate which tend to ensure that the Border Collie dog remains consistent with itself; thus we may breed to lengthen leg-length and find that the tail increases in length as well, staying in proportion to the increase in height gained elsewhere. This self-consistency factor operates on the breeder's side normally, for it enables us to at least make some planned improvements without running the risk of totally losing more than we gain.

5. Genetic ratios are worked on a statistically large population size, and with small breeding programs it may take many matings to achieve the ratio. It is not wise to draw conclusions too quickly. Environmental influences must also be taken into account, e.g. with incorrect feeding a puppy may fail to reach his height or substance potential.

Regression

Where genetic input involves a whole population, each succeeding generation of dogs will be the average of the characteristics of their parents. Thus if a given characteristic is consistently bred for or against it can influence the appearance of the next generation. Consider the dominant characteristic ticking. Continuously breeding the double recessive 'tt' will raise the average of its occurrence (clean white) in future generations until ticking disappears from the breed. However, there are many characteristics in our dogs to be considered. While it is possible to show spectacular results in some areas, particularly phenotype extremes, this is usually at the expense of other characteristics, which at the same time will regress towards the population average. A case in point could be bad temperament. As it is more difficult to 'see' poor temperament in the show ring (or conversely easier to 'hide' it) than it is to spot a dog which 'looks good', it is very easy to see how a

Mating between homozygous black and double recessive chocolate. All puppies black but carry chocolate

population's genetic mean for given characteristics can be affected.

Known gene data

Recessive characteristics

Coat colour

Chocolate—at some stage the gene (B) which causes the normal pigment to be black has mutated to produce brown (b) pigment. Chocolate (brown) occurs in a range of shades from deep rich brown to tan and light tan. Chocolate × Chocolate produces brown puppies (bb) with liver-coloured noses and lighter brown or amber eyes.

• Tricolour—part of the standard agouti series, (a^t) (see page 87). Tricolour appears to be recessive. The tan markings appear on the front and back legs, cheeks, under the tail and as dots above the eyes. The tan may be present at birth or appear gradually within the first week. In the latter instance the tan can usually be found under the tail at first. Tan markings range from rich deep tan to pale lemon and may be seen on black, blue or chocolate dogs.

• Blue—results from a mutant gene of the dilution (D,d) series which affects the spacing of the pigment in the hair follicles: Blue × Blue produces blue puppies (d,d). Blue puppies are often born a light silvery grey and darken with maturity.

• Red/Yellow—in my opinion, this colour in the Border Collie is the result of the Extension series of genes (E,e). If the dog carries the recessive (e,e) the black pigment cannot show up and thus the coat appears red/yellow. However, the existence or non-existence in Border Collies of the alternative red/yellow of the agouti series has not yet, to my knowledge, been proven. Red × Red produces all red puppies. The colour ranges from clear cream to wheaten and 'ginger'. As this gene does not

hound ear

prick ear

rose ear modified

semi-erect ear—pricked,
but modified by a fold

Ear types found in gene pool of Border Collies

affect the nose or eye pigment, a red/yellow from the dominant black will have a black nose and dark brown eyes, while red/yellow from a chocolate dog will have a liver-coloured nose and lighter brown eyes.

• Lilac or silver grey—results from the action of the dilution (d,d) (which also produces blue) on the chocolate coat colour. The pigment granules in the hair follicles of an otherwise chocolate dog will be distributed less densely, or in irregular 'clumps', and the coat will be lilac in appearance. As with the blue, lilac puppies are born very light in colour and darken with maturity. However, the lilac is still a solid colour. The eye and nose pigments tone in with the coat colour.

Coat length

Long hair is the recessive mutation of the gene for short coats. Among Border Collies with the (l,l) recessive for long hair, however, the actual length of hair varies. The Standard calls for a medium-length coat, and my experience has been that most Border Collie breeders

find 'improving the coat' relatively simple to achieve. Medium × Medium coated parents usually maintains correct coat length in puppies; dogs light in coat put to dogs with profuse coats usually improves the coat length in the puppies rather than the reverse, suggesting the influence of polygenes on coat length. Various aspects of the coat including length, texture, thickness and sheen may be influenced by environmental factors such as feeding, grooming and climate.

Wavy or curly coats

A wavy or curly coat is considered to be recessive, but it is not known if more than one gene determines the degree of waviness. Wavy-coatedness is found in the gene pool of the Border Collie.

Blue eye

From my own breeding experience the occurrence of one blue eye (rarely two) can result from matings

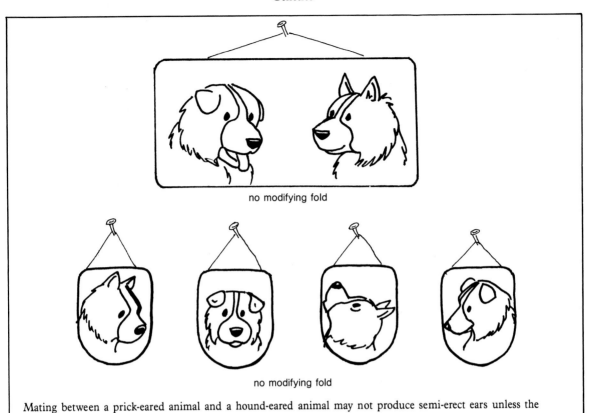

no modifying fold

no modifying fold

Mating between a prick-eared animal and a hound-eared animal may not produce semi-erect ears unless the modifying fold factor is present

between two normally brown-eyed parents. It is usually associated with excess white markings on the head, i.e. a half-white face, and lack of pigment along the eyelid of the blue eye, with normal pigment along the eyelid of the opposite eye and elsewhere. Normally only one puppy is affected in an average sized litter of seven; mating two known carriers increases the incidence to approximately 30 per cent. The genetic determination of the blue eye is not exactly known but some weight is given to the idea that it results from a limited amount of pigment occurring in the eye cells. In my opinion this would be consistent with the method of determination of the white markings. A second suggestion is that it may be linked to the gene for the expression of the merle coat colour.

A blue or 'wall' eye is clearly distinguishable from the normal blue eyes with which all puppies are born. Such 'baby blue' eyes can be seen to darken to tone in with puppy's coat colour as the puppy approaches 8–12 weeks of age.

Pricked ears

Pricked ears are considered to be recessive, but it must be remembered that ear style is determined by a number of independent major genes and possibly a number of polygenes as well. While the placement and strength of the ear ligaments might be such that the ear should stand erect, this must be combined with the correct texture and thickness of the ear leather (fleshy part) for the ear to hold up.

The tendency to a pricked ear is part of the gene pool of the Border Collie; while we might endeavour to breed for the semi-erect ear required by the Standard, the influence of both the small pricked-ear and the large heavy type of ear affects the degree of success possible in stabilising the semi-erect type of ear carriage.

Opinions differ as to what is meant by 'semi-erect', and also whether 'semi-erect' should be the preferred or only acceptable ear-carriage in the Border Collie. Furthermore, it is important to be aware of a dog's true natural ear-carriage when planning breeding programs.

White markings

The occurrence of white markings is a very interesting characteristic whereby the solid colour coat becomes depigmented in a very orderly way. This lack of pigment in the skin and hair follicles is thought to be governed by a series of mutant genes but affected by other modifiers as well. Probably the most reliable way to control the appearance of white markings is to breed towards the population average. The characteristic amount of white markings among Border Collies is known as 'Irish spotting', and is only one step down from a completely self-coloured dog.

Dominant characteristics

Of the following, some characteristics are considered to be major-dominant, while others are affected by polygenes.

Nose pigment

Nose pigment is considered to be determined by a major gene, that for black. However, the black pigment of the nose leather is affected in the same manner as the black pigment of the coat, that is, by the recessives (b) and (d). This means that chocolate dogs have liver-coloured noses and blue dogs have slate-grey noses.

One other consideration to be taken into account in the Border Collie is the occurrence of small patches on the nose which do not completely pigment over. I have not been able to track down the inheritance factor involved in this phenomenon but observation of my own breeding stock has shown up the following:
1. In one particular strain the puppies are often born with some or most of their noses pigmented; usually all have black noses by the age of six weeks. This strain is one which has shown the most tendency to various degrees of black spots occurring, ranging from a few spots on the legs to spots on the white of the muzzle and finally to ticking on the chest.
2. Puppies from my chocolate strain are much slower to express nose pigment, occasionally taking up to the age of twelve to eighteen months.
3. Dogs which lack small patches of nose pigment may breed either way. Unfortunately I am not able to give the ratios in which this occurs.

Eye colour

Eye colour would appear to be dominant for dark brown in the Border Collie. It is known that eye pigment is affected by the (d) and (b) genes, so that blue dogs have light brown to amber eyes and chocolate dogs have lighter brown eyes. The (e) gene does not affect eye colour, so that a red dog will have the dark brown eye of a normally black dog unless of the genotype bbee. In the latter case, the dog is basically a chocolate-pigmented dog affected by the non-extension gene ee, and will have the lighter eye colour and liver pigment of the solid chocolate.

Black coat colour

Black coat is the result of the top dominant gene in the Agouti series (see page 87). This series has been widely studied in other genetic fields, e.g. the rat, so that a number of details about black-coated animals are known. Following are a few points worth considering:
1. The black effect is not a 'colour' at all, but arises from the pigment cells being so closely packed together as to appear a solid colour. The cells have been identified under microscope investigation as having an oval shape and are observedly different from the round 'yellow' pigment cells.
2. A 'range' of black has been observed. This may be due to the effects of polygenes or to the effect of incomplete dominance.
3. (A^s) is affected by the (d), (b) and (e) genes, giving rise to blue, chocolate and red.

Ticking

Ticking is a dominant gene designated (T). It shows up as small black spots on the various white sections of the Border Collie. Mild ticking may be a few spots on the legs, increasing to spots on the white areas of the muzzle, and finally to heavy 'flecking' throughout the white coat and mane. An interesting feature of ticking is that it is not observable at birth and usually shows up when puppies are about 3 months of age, i.e. at the stage of losing baby coat and establishing adult coat. Border Collies free of ticking, known as 'clean cut' markings, would be the recessive (tt). While ticking is a matter of personal preference, it is not a fault and should not be judged as such. Ticking has been part of the gene pool of Border Collies since known development. To only breed (tt) × (tt) could eventually lose this characteristic from the Border Collie's gene pool as the heterozygous (Tt) animals die out.

An interesting feature of ticking is that it requires the presence of the gene for white markings since, without a white face, collar and legs, the ticking would not show up.

Feathering

It is not known whether feathering is inherited as a dominant characteristic in its own right or as a further modification of the (l,l) gene.

Characteristics of uncertain inheritance

There are many other characteristics, both desirable and undesirable, in our dogs which are quite observable but for which the mode of inheritance is not specifically known. These are considered below with whatever information is known or has been observed to date.

Temperament

A dog's temperament is usually described in terms of 'good' (desirable), 'timid' or 'aggressive'. This appears to have a slight heritable factor but it is difficult to observe accurately as it is one of the characteristics most moulded by an animal's environment. For example, a soft-natured puppy which might have developed into a gentle adult may become a timid fear-biter if mistreated as a puppy.

Eating habits

This may seem a strange choice of characteristic to include but a little closer thought will show that this is not so. My observation has been that Border Collies are normally very sensible eaters but that non-interested eaters do show familial links. Furthermore, some Border Collies will show a definite preference to be with their owners or to be 'doing something' rather than eat. Bush lore has it that these types of puppies make the best workers, and are the most loyal and biddable adults. Again, it is sometimes difficult to know how much fussiness in eating is the result of environmental factors, but my own observation of many litters has shown that there is usually at least one in the litter which will ignore the food dish for something more interesting.

Dewclaws

Dewclaws are the expression of a fifth digit on either the front or hind legs, or both. Dew claws are certainly a heritable condition but their occurrence is so infrequent among Border Collies that few observations have been made. Another restricting factor is that if they do appear they are normally removed from the hind legs two or three days after birth, thus few owners are ever aware that their puppy was born with dew claws.

Cryptorchidism

This refers to the condition where either one or both testicles fail to descend into the scrotum in a male dog. The condition is considered to be hereditary but dominance or recessiveness is not known. The condition has been strongly observed to be familial, i.e. known to persistently occur among the members of a given family group. Most geneticists strongly recommend that animals from affected familial groups should not be used in breeding as this appears to concentrate the polygenes involved and the incidence of affected animals is increased. The recommendation includes females of the family group as well, for though they cannot 'show' the problem they can still carry and transfer the predisposition for the problem.

Umbilical hernia

A softish lump in the area of the umbilical cord. Not a common problem in Border Collies but is considered to be familial in occurrence.

Epilepsy

Again, not common in Border Collies but it does occasionally occur. It is considered to be hereditary but affected by environmental stimulus.

Hip dysplasia

A defect where the hip bone (femur) does not fit properly into its socket. It is considered heritable and affected dogs should not be used for breeding.

Incorrect bite

A condition which occurs when the lower jaw is of incorrect length or shape. It has been observed to occur in related animals but the exact method of inheritance is not known. It is considered the breeding with affected animals would lead to an increase of affected animals.

Ceroid-lipofusinosis (CL)

(Sometimes referred to as 'storage disease'.)

This condition occurs as a result of a build-up of pigment in parts of the dog's body, but most especially in the nerve cells. The condition manifests itself as a change in behaviour of the dog towards indiscriminate aggression and biting, blindness and instability in movement. As a result most affected dogs either die or are put down by the age of two years. Though information regarding this condition has only recently become available, it is at this stage considered heritable.

It is suggested that neither dogs nor bitches should be used for breeding before the age of two years, by which time the disease will normally have been detected in affected animals. However, it is very important to be fully aware that an animal, male or female, can be a carrier of CL although they themselves have not suffered from the disease. Such carriers can still pass on the disease to their offspring if mated with another carrier.

Assistance in determining whether an animal is a potential carrier or not may be obtained from the breed club in most states.

Genetics and breeding programs

So far we have been considering some of the known genetic material relevant to the Border Collie. The next logical step would be to apply this information to some form of breeding program. As this is a complicated and contentious area, the reader is advised to consult further. The following very brief remarks are offered as a starting point:

1. Clearly fix in your mind the type of Border Collie you would like to become known as 'your' bloodline.

2. Choose your own parameters, i.e. choose which aspects of the Border Collie you will never sacrifice and which you may be prepared to waive occasionally. Thus, you may choose never to breed from any animal which is not absolutely sound in movement. On the other hand, you may always seek to achieve full collars, but be prepared to accept a half-collar if the animal fulfils the movement requirements.

3. Put virility and fertility high on your list of priorities, also the ability to copulate and to whelp and raise puppies without difficulties. It makes sense that a breed will ultimately decline if numbers are reduced through such factors as poor fertility or whelping problems.

4. Remember to outcross strategically. The 'loss of hybrid vigour' ('inbreeding depression') is a very real phenomenon. Constant inbreeding brings undesirable, normally recessive, characteristics to homozygosity. The lesson from nature indicates that heterozygosity over the majority of characteristics is the more favoured situation.

5. Always accept your responsibility as a breeder and remember that we are all only custodians of this beautiful breed. It belongs just as much to the future as it does to us today. Make sure you deliver into the future a Border Collie to be proud of.

Results of colour matings

1. Wheaten male of black and white parents to wheaten female of black and white parents.
Progeny: all wheaten (red).

2. Wheaten pup from above litter mated to a black and white dog in 1984 produced an interesting result.
Progeny: 1 black/white, 2 tricolours, 3 wheaten/reds.

The result of this mating would prove the existence of (ee) yellow since the black/white male must have the genotype $(A^s a^t Ee)$. That is, he cannot be carrying (A^y) since we know he is carrying tricolour but is himself black/white. If he were $(A^y a^t)$ he would have to be yellow, as (A^y) is dominant to (a^t).

On the other hand, the bitch could be $(A^y a^t E)$ as she is yellow throwing tricolour, or $(A^s a^t ee)$ which is also the yellow phenotype throwing tricolour.

The $(A^y a^t E)$ tricolour mating would be expected to yield the ratio of 4 black/white, 2 yellow, 2 tricolour.

The $(A^s a^t ee)$ tricolour mating would yield the ratio 3 black/white, 4 yellow and 1 tricolour.

A larger number of matings would be required before a pattern could be determined.

3. Wheaten (red) male to chocolate bitch.
Progeny: 7 black/white puppies.

All that can be concluded so far is that (ee) yellows exist in the breed. We have not yet disproved the existence of (y) yellows. Both yellows can and do exist together in other breeds, but this is the exception rather than the rule. As far as I can see this could only be proved by a 'chance' mating between 2 yellows which produces an all black/white litter.

4. Black/white male to black/white bitch.
Progeny: included a chocolate/tricolour dog.

5. Chocolate male to red bitch.
Progeny: 3 black/white, 3 tricolours, 1 blue.

6. Chocolate male carrying blue and tricolour to black/white bitch carrying tricolour.
Progeny: black/white, blue tricolour (tan markings), chocolate tricolour (tan markings), lilac/white.

The author would appreciate any other test mating results from breeders willing to add their knowledge to that known so far regarding the genotype of the Border Collie. This invitation applies to other characteristics as well as colour.

7 Potted History of the Modern Border Collie

As with most modern breeds of dogs the true history of the Border Collie's evolution is lost in obscurity. All dogs are of mixed ancestry and all are considered to have evolved from a primitive animal such as the wolf, jackal or coyote, with most scientists now favouring the wolf. This is borne out by studies revealing that the wolf and the dog have the same chromosome count (78). The Australian Dingo, regarded as one of the few remaining truly wild dogs, also attests to the dog's adaptation from the wolf. Despite early claims in canine literature (particularly with regard to the development of the Australian Red Kelpie), it has now been proved that the fox is not related to the wolf, and since the fox has a different chromosome count to the dog it is considered that matings between the two would be highly unlikely to take place or to produce viable offspring.

Selective breeding over thousands of years moulded the wolf into the ancestor of the domestic dog. It is considered that some of our modern sheepdog breeds can trace their ancestry back for 3000 years, thus firmly establishing the traits of tractability and shepherding.

It should be remembered that the Border Collie is first and foremost a sheepdog. There are probably still more Borders out doing a day's work on farms and in stockyards across Australia than are to be found as pets, show or obedience dogs. Indeed, it is this combination of tractability and biddability that has resulted in the Border being the great all-rounder that he is. It is a tribute to the Border's character that he takes on each role so successfully and with apparent ease.

The modern development of the dog we know as the Border Collie in Australia really took place in two stages: firstly as a result of the early importation into Australia of working sheepdogs and secondly with the drawing up of the early Standards for the breed.

Early importations

The development of the Border Collie is clearly allied to the development of Australia itself and indeed is intricately bound up with the development of his workmates the Australian Cattle Dog and the Australian Kelpie. During the late 1800s and early 1900s the leading pastoralists were men of enterprise from Scotland and England who were opening up the land and developing our primary industries. It is possible to imagine that these farmers hailed from a long line of farming families who were accustomed to the use of dogs for shepherding. Records show that sending for sheepdogs from the old country was quite a common practice. Working sheepdogs were thus brought in to assist in the running of their huge sheep and cattle runs but it was not long before the pull of competition began to assert itself and Sheep Dog Trials became a well established way of showing what a good dog could do.

These early arrivals were not known exclusively as Border Collies, but more commonly as working sheepdogs, described in many instances as black and tan, black and white or splotchy blue, having pricked ears and rather short coats, and were usually described as 'big dogs'.

The early history of the Border Collie is inextricably bound up with the development of good strains of working sheepdogs in Great Britain, about which there is a dearth of written records available. The 'Border' as such is variously known as both 'Welsh' and 'Scottish'; the designation 'Border' being used to refer to dogs from the region between England and Scotland. The word referring to the dog seems to have first slipped into our vocabulary about 1907, but it was not in common usage in Great Britain until much later.

An early Royal Show, possibly 1950. Mrs Mollie Cleary heads the line-up (left) with her bitch Farmborough, considered the first Border Collie in New South Wales to become a Champion under the newly established regulations

These early dogs were imported to work and their survival depended upon their gradually being bred to fit the Australian conditions. Some of the adaptations required were aimed at increasing stamina and endurance levels because of the large size of farms and distances to be covered when droving; improving the ability to withstand heat and harsh, dry conditions; and giving increased protection against grass seeds, dust and torrential rain.

Thus, the beautiful, versatile, hard-working Australian Border Collie gradually took shape. Analogous to the Border's development were the development of the Kelpie and Blue Heeler Cattle dogs, when a hardier, short-coated dog was required to work large runs of sheep in the outback, and a tougher, more aggressive dog was needed for cattle. The Kelpie is also believed to derive from imported working sheepdogs from Great Britain selectively bred for certain desirable characteristics. When a tough hardy dog was required for cattle work, a smooth-coated blue merle dog was crossed with a dingo, then selectively bred and refined to produce the now famous Blue Heeler.

Establishing a Standard

The evolution of the modern pure bred Border Collie occurred gradually and in different places. Over the years instances have been recorded of dogs competing in sheepdog trials being exhibited in conformation classes at the same time. It seems that during the 1920s to the 1940s some of the Agricultural Show Societies began bench classes for dogs, but at this time there were very few state controlling bodies and no National Kennel Council. Some people simply considered their working dogs well worth showing in the Any Other Variety classes.

During the latter part of the 1940s and early 1950s several states independently drew up a standard for the breed and began issuing challenge certificates. However, in New South Wales in 1953 the Australian Cattle Dog, Australian Kelpie and Border Collie were formalised into a group known as the Australian Working Dog Group, obviously recognising the three breeds as significant to the development of Australian primary industry and

Foundation dogs of the Nidgee Kennels: Ch. Nidgee King on the left, Ch. Farmborough on the right (pet name Lucky); Nidgee Right Bower (puppy)

possibly also as Australia's own breeds. The dogs on which the early Standards were based were those bred and developed here over some forty years, though as already noted they had their ancestry in imported working sheepdogs. The Border Collie as such was not benched in Great Britain during this time.

In 1963 the Australian National Kennel Control approved and adopted a national Standard for the Border Collie, thus establishing the Border as a breed type for the future. Great Britain gave recognition to the Border as a Bench dog in 1976 and gave it Championship status in 1982. The old Australian Working Dog Group grew into what is now known as the Working Dog Group, though many show societies and kennel clubs still continue to award the Best Australian Working Dog.

This is a very abbreviated history of the way in which this magnificent breed became recognised and established as a pure breed dog. There are, though, three points I would like to make for consideration:

1. The Border Collie is inextricably bound to his working forebears and this is as it should remain. The Border should always be able to 'earn a day's pay' as

Ch. Lucky Rex (born 1950), stud dog of the Yenching Kennels

Ch. Wyena King (born 1956) was used extensively in the early 1960s to produce the foundation stock of many major kennels

On the right is Ch. Margian Spats (born 1964), winner of 3 Challenges and 1 Reserve Challenge at Sydney Royal shows, with his daughter Ch. Margian Serella (born 1966), winner of 1 Challenge and 1 Reserve Challenge at Sydney Royal shows

Ch. Dawnell Mie (born 1967) as a puppy with his sire Ch. Storm Major (born 1965) on the right

Ch. Dawnell Mie, winner of 4 Challenges and 1 Reserve Challenge, Sydney Royal shows

A "TRUSTY" FELLOW
AUST CHAMP 1969

KAIAPOI ARANUI

Ch. Kaiapoi Aranui (born 1964). Photo captioned by his proud owner

Left: Ch. Ebony Velvet (born 1971). At least six major kennels throughout Australia can trace their foundations back to this bitch or her progeny

a working dog and it is the responsibility of breeders, judges and owners to ensure that this remains so. In my opinion to judge to the Standard is consistent with maintaining the Border as a working dog.

2. It is interesting to note that the Australian Cattle Dog, Australian Kelpie and the (Australian) Border Collie have a commonality of ancestry, thus highlighting how breeders can alter the appearance of a 'dog type'.

3. Because of the very recent changes to the Standard to include additional colours it needs to be pointed out that a variety of colours always existed in the breed, not only in their working sheepdog ancestry but also in the early benched dogs. Written records make reference to liver and white, black and tans, blue merles, sable and sandy coloured dogs, as well as to tricolours and black and white. It would seem to have been the whim of breeders of the late 1940s and early 1950s to cull for the black and white dogs which have become the hallmark of the breed.

(*Note:* The nomenclature of colour, unfortunately, is not consistent. Liver is probably what would be regarded today as chocolate while it is considered that the reference to merle was not, in fact, true merle but what is now known as blue.)

The first Standard set in Australia

Head: Skull flat and tapering towards the eyes, slight stop, cheeks flat and clean, muzzle balances skull, nose black.

Teeth: 20 top, 22 bottom, sound and strong with scissor-like action, the lower incisors just behind but touching the upper, over or undershot a bad fault.

Eyes: Medium brown, set obliquely and almond shape.

Expression: Alert, keen, intelligent.

Ears: Small, not set too closely, semi or rose.

Body: Should be rather long with well sprung ribs, chest deep, loins slightly arched and powerful.

Legs: Forelegs straight and muscular, with a fair amount of bone, pasterns flexible without weakness. Hindlegs muscular at thighs, moderately bent stifle and strong hock.

Feet: Are to be oval in shape, toes arched and close together, soles well padded.

Tail: Medium long with brush when carried quite low with slight swirl, never over the back.

Coat: Double, the outer coat of long hair with dense undercoat with abundant frill and mane, forelegs well feathered, hindlegs above hocks profusely covered but smooth below, face smooth.

Height: Approximately 18" bitches, dogs 20".

Weight: 28 lbs to 32.

Colour: Black and white, black and tan and white, black and tan.

Bibliography

Ascroft, P. *The Border Collie*, Times Longbooks, 1965

Ash, E.C. *The Practical Dog Book*, Simpkin Marshall Ltd, 1930

Bray, J. & Brack, L. *'Good Dog': A Guide for the Beginner*, Kangaroo Press, Sydney 1991

Hart, A. *Dog Owner's Encyclopaedia of Veterinary Medicine*, TFH Publications, 1971

Hartley, C.W.G. *The Shepherd's Dogs*, 3rd ed, Whitcombe and Tombs, 1972

Kaleski, R. *Australian Barkers and Biters*, The Endeavour Press, 1914

Kelley, R.B. *Sheep Dogs*, 4th ed, Angus & Robertson, Sydney, 1970

Kennel Control Council (Victoria) *Dogs of Australia*, Humphries & Formula Press

Longton, T. & Hart, E. *The Sheep Dog*, David & Charles Inc., 1976

McDowell-Lyons, *The Dog in Action*, 7th ed., Howell Book House Inc., 1985

MacLeod, N. *The Australian Kelpie Handbook*, 2nd ed, self-published, 1985

Moore, J.L. *The Canine King*, Standard Newspapers Ltd, 1929

Richardson, E. *Forty Years with Dogs*, Hutchinson & Co. Ltd

Robinson, R. *Genetics for Dog Breeders*, Pergamon Press, 1982

Srb, A., Owen, R. & Edgar, R. *General Genetics*, 2nd ed, W.H. Freeman & Co.

Spira, H. *Canine Terminology*, Harper & Row, 1982

Suzuki, D. & Griffiths, A. *An Introduction to Genetic Analysis*, W.H. Freeman & Co.

Tuck Nichols, V. *How to Show Your Own Dog*, TFH Publications, 1969

Vidler, P. *The Border Collie in Australia*, Gotrah Enterprises, 1983

Wentworth-Day, J. *The Wisest Dog in the World*, W.S. Cains Ltd

Index